COME BACK, MOSES, WE NEED YOU

some jottings on

Twelve Psalms
Isaiah 1-12
Exodus 34:5-7

Stephen B Dawes

Southleigh Publications

Text copyright © Stephen B Dawes 1998

The author asserts the moral right to be identified
as the author of this work

Published by
Southleigh Publications
4 Upland Crescent
Truro
Cornwall TR1 1LU

ISBN 0 9520644 8 0

First edition 1998

All rights reserved

Acknowledgements
The chapters on Psalms first appeared in the Methodist Recorder
from September 1997 to August 1998
The chapter on Isaiah 1-12 first appeared in "Guidelines", January -
April 1996 pp50-69, published by the Bible Reading Fellowship
Both are reproduced with permission

A catalogue record for this book
is available from the British Library

Printed by
Mid-Cornwall Printing
Newham
Truro

Dear Reader

Thank you for buying this little book which is a collection of Old Testament jottings from three different places. The studies on Psalms 1, 8, 18, 19, 24, 42, 51, 82, 100, 103, 131 and 150 were published in the *Methodist Recorder* from September 1997 to August 1998. The notes on Isaiah 1-12 come from the January-April 1996 issue of *Guidelines*, the Bible Study Notes published by the Bible Reading Fellowship. The last chapter on Exodus 34:5-7 - which is at the heart of the Old Testament and from which the title of the book is taken - is part of a set of lecture notes.

I am grateful to Moira Sleight, the editor of the *Methodist Recorder*, for permission to reproduce the articles from the *Recorder* in this form.

I am grateful too to Richard Fisher and the *Bible Reading Fellowship* for permission to reproduce the notes from *Guidelines*. It is always a pleasure to be asked to write for *Guidelines* - a series which has been described as BRF's best kept secret. Far be it from a regular contributor to commend the series, but I do and do so most warmly. I had hoped to include here some recent notes on 1 Samuel 1-16 and Judges 1-8 but space didn't permit. Hopefully there might be a volume 2 of these jottings: but you can always read the originals in *Guidelines* ...

Finally, I must express my gratitude to the Principal, staff and students of the South West Ministry Training Course and the Department of Continuing and Adult Education of the University of Exeter for allowing me to continue to teach Old Testament. I am sure the Principal would have given permission to reproduce the lecture notes on Exodus 34 - but I didn't ask.

Rev Dr Stephen B Dawes

Chairman of the Cornwall District of the Methodist Church

CONTENTS

Psalm 1	7
Psalm 8	10
Psalm 18	13
Psalm 19	16
Psalm 24	19
Psalm 42	21
Psalm 51	24
Psalm 82	27
Psalm 100	30
Psalm 103	33
Psalm 131	36
Psalm 150	39
Isaiah 1-12	43
The Bible Reading Fellowship	66
Exodus 34:5-7	67

PSALM 1

A book for all seasons

In 516 BC the Jerusalem Publishing House published the *Book of Praises* for use in the new Temple, built to celebrate the return of the Jews from exile in Babylon. We still use it today, though we call it the *Book of Psalms*. Like any other hymnbook it contains a variety of hymns, long and short, old and new and, dare I say it, good and bad. It includes songs of praise and thanksgiving, confessions of sin, anguished cries for help, prayers for the king and the nation and even some violent outbursts against God. Most of its hymns are for public worship, either in ordinary services or for specials, but some are better suited to private prayer and meditation. There are also anthems for choirs and words for worship events for which we haven't got the rest of the instructions and so we have to imagine the actions which were taking place. Some of this worship material was already ancient by the time this new book was published, some was decidedly modern. It was gathered from various places and for some of the hymns we have the names of authors, arrangers or compilers, while others are anonymous. Some of it even comes complete with musical directions and the name of the tune to be used.

We can find all human life in the words of these hymns, its good and bad, its beauty and tragedy, its hopes and fears. Many of the pictures of God and his love in the psalms have been taken up by later hymnwriters to become familiar parts of our worship today: but there are also the nasty bits. In its service book the Church of England puts some verses of some of the psalms in square brackets, so that congregations of a sensitive or squeamish disposition needn't sing them. Our versions of the psalms in *Hymns and Psalms* usually miss those sort of verses out altogether. It is helpful if we remember here that hymns and psalms, as well as prayers and all the language we use in worship, is poetry rather than prose. It is also helpful if we can accept that feelings of hate, rage, anger and despair are real and that even religious people feel them from time to time or in particular circumstances. The compilers of the Book of Psalms evidently believed that such feelings could and should be expressed in worship, and that God was big enough to cope with them. So do I.

Most hymn books contain some hymns which become classics and others which have a mercifully short life, but both Judaism and Christianity decided early on that the complete Book of Psalms was much more than the hymnbook of the second temple. So they have handed this anthology of religious poetry down to us as a classic of spirituality and theology which has something to give to the people of God everywhere and for ever. That is how I hope we can approach the twelve psalms I have selected for us to study, beginning with Psalm 1.

Whether Psalm 1 is the first psalm by design or accident we will never know. It is anonymous and has no title, but it provocatively sets the scene for the hymnbook as a whole. It boldly points out that there are two ways of life, a good one and a bad one, and that those who choose God's way find their lives blessed and those who make the wrong choice find their lives blighted. I say "provocatively" because some psalms strongly question this idea, voicing the cries of faithful people who are suffering because of their faithfulness and who see the prosperity of the wicked all around. Other psalms support it, not least Psalm 37 where the writer says that he has never seen the righteous suffering nor their children begging bread, which makes me wonder where has he been all his life. Psalm 1 boldly and baldly expresses the orthodox theology of the Old Testament, that in this life righteousness is rewarded and wickedness is punished. This has left a dangerous legacy, seen in the angry or resigned question that every minister has faced at some time in a pastoral tragedy, "What have I done to deserve this?" So it is popular today to dismiss this idea, just as parts of the Old Testament dismiss it, but maybe we should be cautious. That goodness is rewarded and wrongdoing is punished is a very rough-and-ready generalisation, but maybe there is enough truth in it to make us stop and think. And if it only reminds us that there is such a thing as corporate or individual wrongdoing - no matter how hopelessly old-fashioned and moralistic that word sounds - and that wrongdoing does have nasty consequences, not necessarily for the perpetrators but certainly for others, then perhaps it is worthwhile listening to? That is certainly what Psalm 1 encourages us to do.

The psalm begins with a translation problem. Are those who make the right choice "happy" (GNB, NRSV, REB) or are they "blessed" (AV, RSV, NIV, NJB)? I prefer "blessed" because "happy" sounds trivial and "blessed" suggests something deeper. After all, we can cope with unhappinesses in our lives if we are sustained by a deeper blessing: but if we are unhappy we cannot be happy. But that leaves the problem that "blessed" isn't contemporary English. Any suggestions for a modern improvement on "happy"? We have the same problem in the Beatitudes and a consistent translation will use the same English word in both places - NRSV and REB fail the test.

The psalmist calls those who make the wrong choice and choose the wrong path "the wicked", "sinners" and "scoffers". The first two of these are common Bible words, but the third is unusual. It is almost a technical term in the "wisdom" literature for those who never listen and who talk big and freely, especially about things they know little about. Other translations call these people "the scornful", "the insolent", "cynics", "mockers" or "those who have no use for God". They are obviously no new phenomenon. The psalmist observes that they might make a lot of noise but their lives fail to blossom into usefulness, they make no contribution to society and in the end they are like chaff blown away in the wind.

By contrast those who are blessed because they have made the right choice and chosen the right path live useful and fruitful lives, like fruit-trees planted in well-irrigated places. People acknowledge their real contribution to the wellbeing of the community and God himself looks approvingly on the way they live. And this blessedness comes from taking proper notice of God's "Torah", his teaching and guidance. Most translations have his "law" here, and that is a pity because "Law" is a very negative word for Christians. We contrast "law" with "gospel" and it makes us think of a religion of duty in which we have to keep commandments in order to pass God's test. In the Old Testament and in Judaism "Torah" means nothing like that at all - read Psalm 119 if you don't believe me.

Psalm 1 may overstate its case. Maybe it doesn't tell it exactly as it is. But its faith and assurance/trust gives us a hope in God to sing about.

PSALM 8

Second in Command

"O LORD, our Lord,
how majestic is your name in all the earth!"

Psalm 8 begins and ends with this shout of praise, but it is not only a psalm in praise of God but also in praise of humanity. God's majestic splendour is beyond words to express. It overshadows the midday sun and makes the night sky pale into insignificance: but instead of dwarfing human beings it makes them stand tall and honoured! Human beings reflect God's majesty. That is the amazing-but-true theme of Psalm 8. The psalm is short, profound, contemporary and, with one exception, simple.

We must pause for a moment at the first line of its opening and closing acclamation, which presents a little teaser for translations. The *New Jerusalem Bible* has "Yahweh, our Lord", which is nearly what the Hebrew is, except that it never writes out the divine name in full nor ever pronounces it. The Hebrew Bible and Jewish tradition always substitutes the word "Lord" for the divine name, in both writing and speech, and the fact that *NJB* breaks with that ancient tradition is its major flaw. The traditional translation, "O LORD, our Lord", follows the Hebrew practice and is about the best we can do. So wherever you see "LORD" in capital letters in our Bibles, as here, you know that the Hebrew has God's unpronounceable name at that point. "LORD, our sovereign" with NRSV and REB would be passable if they translated "Lord" as "sovereign" every time, which they don't, and about the worst is "O LORD, our Governor" which is used in *Hymns and Psalms* and reminds me of *Porridge*.

Verse 2 is obscure. It is not clear where it starts or where the lines divide, let alone what they mean. If you want to pursue that further just look at six different translations and you'll see how they all treat it differently. Speculations and suggestions abound, but because that's all they are and because there is plenty more to think about in the psalm I am going to leave it at that.

Verses 3 and 4 ask a question in good Hebrew poetic style. English poetry used to have rhyme and metre; Hebrew poetry has "parallelism". It says things twice. So the second part of verse 4 where God's "care" for "mortals" parallels his "being mindful of" the same "human beings" in the first part. The question is, compared with the sun, moon and stars, where do human beings fit in? The answer we expect is - nowhere at all, they are too insignificant to count. Notice how the question re-emphasises God's splendour, the heavens are not the work of God's hands, merely of his "fingers". The moon and the stars are not eternal and independent powers or "gods", as they were to some of Israel's ancient neighbours, but tools forged by God and set in place by him. For those who sang this psalm, there was only one God and he was the creator and sustainer of absolutely everything. And if human beings are nothing compared with the moon and stars, they must be less than nothing compared with the God whose fingers shaped the heavens.

Wrong! says verse 5. God has actually made human beings only a "little lower" than either God himself, or a god, or the angels or the heavenly beings which surround God's throne. Or a little less than divine. All those translations are possible, for the word used is the one usually translated as God, god or gods and occasionally used of angels or even mighty heroes. Whichever you prefer the meaning is clear enough, as the following verses spell out. Humanity has been "crowned with glory and honour" and given "dominion" over everything. There is a clear link here with the creation story in Genesis 1 where human beings are made "in the image of God", a phrase which means that we are entrusted by God with his authority to continue his creative work. This position is not one of crude power to exploit the world of nature and impose our will on it, though that is often what we have done, but one of trust, authority and stewardship as God's representatives. So what about Dolly the Sheep? We were told, when she first appeared, that it was a dangerous thing when humans started "playing God". Psalm 8 and Genesis 1 unite in saying that "playing God" is exactly what God wants us to do. Of course we can get it wrong. Of course our arrogance, selfishness and greed can foul things up. Of course we can misuse our power and abuse our stewardship. But the answer is not to stop being stewards but to be good ones. We cannot abdicate our responsibility to shape and mould creation. God has taken the risk in giving that to us and saying, "No, thank you", is not an option.

And finally to its title. NRSV has "To the leader; according to The Gittith". This is probably an instruction to the Director of Music that this psalm is to be sung to the tune, "The Gittith", though it is just possible that a *gittith* is a musical instrument. The second part, "A psalm of David", could mean a number of things: that David wrote it ("By David"), or that the psalm was part of the royal collection in David's Temple which the Babylonians had destroyed in 586 BC ("Belonging to the royal Temple") or that it is dedicated to the king ("For David", ie "For the King of David's line"). I'll leave that until next chapter when we look at Psalm 18.

PSALM 18

Truly death-defying

Let's start at the beginning of this psalm with its long title which says precisely when David first sang this psalm. This seems to confirm that the phrase, "a Psalm of David", means that he wrote it, which is how GNB always translates it in Psalms. But in the first verse of the Song of Songs, where the same expression is used about Solomon, it adds a footnote, "By Solomon; or dedicated to Solomon, or about Solomon". Why is it so coy in Psalms? Obviously, you might think, because 14 psalms give a time and place in David's life when he did it! But then you see that the classic Jewish commentary on Psalms made around 750 AD does that to almost all of the 73 "Psalms of David". It seems that there was a growing tradition of ascribing psalms to David, with imaginative scholars competing to find the places in his life where each psalm could fit best. That ought to make us cautious. In Methodist circles the Davidic authorship of all the psalms attributed to him was questioned as long ago as 1822 by Adam Clarke, thrice President of the Conference, in his widely read *Bible Commentary*. Few scholars today think that David wrote many, if any, of the psalms and even fewer think that the question is important. It might be interesting to read the author's name and date under a hymn in *Hymns and Psalms*, but what matters is what a hymn says and what it does to us as we sing it. So with this magnificent psalm. And that is my last word in this series on who wrote any of the psalms we shall look at.

Psalm 18 is passionate, dramatic and triumphant. Too much so for modern tastes, some will say. It is also intensely personal. Like Wesley's personal hymns it gives me words to celebrate "my" deliverence and to give "my" testimony to the great things God has done for "me". It is an intense psalm of personal thanksgiving to God who has "saved me from my enemies". Strong stuff. Vivid metaphors. Powerful pictures. It sees existence and faith as a life and death struggle. Good versus evil. Light versus darkness. Faith versus unbelief. Humility versus pride. It may have started life as a Royal Psalm written to celebrate a national victory and to be spoken by the king, but in the Temple hymnbook it becomes a victory song for anyone to use. It praises God for rescuing me from my enemies, but before we say that it then lets itself down by gloating over these defeated enemies we need to have a closer look at these enemies who appear in verse 2 and keep on cropping up in the psalms.

Think of it like this. In a world where life was often "nasty, brutal and short" you lived in constant insecurity. Life was always under threat. It might be from hunger or sickness, poverty or famine, marauding foreigners or nasty neighbours. You lived a marginal life in a vulnerable little nation in a big and hostile world. The great enemy was "Death" whose powers were felt in all sorts of ways. So the psalmist praises God for saving him from the great enemy, Death, from its underworld waters and the darkness of the kingdom of "Sheol".

There are two quite different ways of looking at death in the Old Testament. One is where death comes at its proper time, when someone dies peacefully in old age having lived out their full life. Here those who die are "gathered to their people", and their relatives though obviously grieving can rejoice over a life "faithfully lived and peacefully died". So "Abraham breathed his last and died in a good old age, an old man and full of years, and was gathered to his people" (Genesis 25:8). His sons bury him and life goes on. This is the "kind and gentle death" of St Francis of Assisi's hymn. Psalm 18 sees death differently. It is vicious, terrifying and completely negative. It leads those forces of evil which are always trying to destroy, hurt and deface what is beautiful, good and healthy. Death is like a huge octopus living in a pit, who is always trying to reach out and catch passers-by with its tentacles and drag them down into darkness and destruction, drowning them in its watery cavern. This is Psalm 18's view of death. Verses 4-5 speak vividly of illness, disaster or suffering of any kind as symptoms of death trying to get its grip on the living.

But the psalmist can testify that God is stronger still and verses 7-15 are a good example of "theophany" language which speaks of God appearing in a terrifying storm (see also Exodus 19:16-20, Judges 5:4-5, Psalms 68:7-9 and 97:1-5).

What are we to make of this powerful military imagery? Do we put it behind us as an example of religious ideas whose day is long gone? Do we take it up as a manifesto for a new militant faith for a new millenium? Hopefully we will do neither. The language may be far from anything in our experience but the message is that God's love and goodness is ultimate and real; that we have a sure and certain hope, which is that the final victory is love's and that in the end God's kingdom will come and his will be done. Here then is an ancient word of reassurance. Malice, evil and death are nigh, but God is nigher! He "redeems" us from these things. He saves, rescues and delivers us from all this shadow side of life. He is our protector, saviour, deliverer, liberator. The psalmist recognises the shadow side of life, and sees it as an enemy: but at the same time he knows it to be a defeated enemy. Every recovery from illness, every problem faced and solved, and every trouble lived through is a victory of life over death. God is on the side of life, he is supremely the "Lord of Life and Conqueror of Death" and "our help in every time of trouble" as we say in Funeral services. And in the end, if not in the meantime, we shall know it to be so. As the hymn puts it so well,

> "Sin and death and hell shall never,
> O'er us final triumph gain;
> God is love, so Love for ever
> O'er the universe must reign".

This positive and confident attitude is seen in the popular Jewish toast and greeting, "leChaim", "To Life". In that word with its hope and defiance of death, there is a whole creed and celebration of the victory of God over death, no matter how strong, terrifying and real the forces of death seem to be.

PSALM 19

For a lazy choir

In the Midrash Ma'arabi this short psalm is entitled, "For a Lazy Choir. Observations". It divides into three parts. The first tells of what the psalmist has learned by observing the day and night skies. The second talks about observing God's "Law". The third is a simple prayer.

Unlike many of us for much of the time, this psalmist goes around with eyes open. But he is more than a careful observer of the natural world. He looks and thinks about what he sees. From the skies and the canopy of space (the "firmament") he concludes that God is; and that he is "glorious". The skies at night and by day may be silent, but they are eloquent. The sun's splendour points beyond itself to its Maker. So the psalmist gives us a song of praise to the Creator God, and in it invites us too to see God's "glory", his splendour, power and mystery, visible in the world he has made (compare Romans 1:20).

These ideas are similar to those we saw in Psalm 8 but very different from those of Psalm 18. In that one the world was a frightening place, stalked by death and inhabited by hostile forces human and otherwise. That psalmist cried out to God as Saviour from life's terrors. There is none of that here. Psalm 19 comes out of the "Wisdom" tradition of ancient Israel, which generally breathes a calm, relaxed and positive attitude to life and faith. Which speaks of and to the real world? Perhaps both. There are times when our world feels like that of Psalm 18, and we cry out to God to save us. At other times it feels like that of Psalm 19, and we praise God for the life he has given.

Part two, verses 7-13, is about observing the "Law" and gives us a song in praise of God who makes himself known in his *Torah*. As the sun gives light and life to the earth, so *Torah* gives light and life to humanity. This key Old Testament word can be translated in various ways - "teaching", "guidance" or "law", for example - and this psalm shows what a warm word it is. There is nothing of cold or calculating legalism in the word at all. It speaks, first and foremost, of God's grace, gift and guidance. So lazy choirs can sing gratefully of this gift of God in a mere seven verses while more conscientious ones can tackle Psalm 119, the longest psalm in the hymnbook, which is entirely devoted to a celebration of *Torah*.

Verses 7-9 are a good example of "parallelism" with each half verse saying the same thing in different words but each repetition adding something more to the meaning of the whole. Try setting them out in three columns. The first set of parallels is a list of different terms for God's instructions: *torah*, decrees, precepts, commandments, fear, ordinances. The fifth one stands out as a bit odd and it can only mean taking respectful notice of what God has said. Elsewhere in the wisdom literature the motto phrase "the fear of the Lord" is best translated into English by the word "religion" - though no translations ever do. The second set of parallels are the adjectives which describe those instructions: perfect, sure, right, clear, pure and true. The third set shows what those instructions do: they revive the soul, make wise the simple, rejoice the heart, enlighten the eyes, endure for ever and are entirely effective.

This life-enhancing purpose of God's teaching is clear in the Ten Commandments. The story is about God rescuing his people from slavery in Egypt, guiding them through the desert and preparing them to enter the Promised Land. God gives them these Commandments *after* they have been rescued. So it is not a matter of, "If you keep these commandments I will rescue you". Instead, as the introduction in Exodus 20:2 shows, it is "I have rescued you, and here's the way to enjoy your new life to the full". Encouraged by God's love which they have experienced in what he has done and equipped by his advice his people can enter the Promised Land. *Torah* is therefore not just good advice. It is good news. It is gospel.

Verses 10-13 need to be printed together without the line which appears between verses 10 and 11 in my NRSV. They speak of the value of this advice in four different ways. It is worth more than gold. It is as sweet as honey. It is a necessary warning. It is advice which, if followed, does lead to a happy life. Verses 12-13 point out just how much we need such advice, for we are all very good at deceiving ourselves and need all the help we can get from either being led astray by the clever talk of the arrogant opinion-formers ("the proud" - remember Psalm 1) or by the nastier side of our own selves (our "wilful sins"). The first is the better translation.

The psalm ends with the prayer often used before Anglican sermons, a practice Methodists would do well to copy. It asks that by the strength of God, the rock foundation of the universe, our lives might match our praises. That by the help of God, who shows us the way and helps us to walk in it, we might live in the light of the truths we believe.

Psalm 19 speaks of God as our Creator and our Redeemer - both/and not either/or and that's a lesson in itself. Not for nothing did C S Lewis call it the greatest poem in the Psalter and one of the greatest lyrics in the world.

PSALM 24

Procession of worshippers

Verse 1 boldly declares that "The earth is the LORD's" and makes a splendid call to worship for a Harvest Festival or Social Responsibility service. God is. There is no other. He alone is the life-giver. He is the world's creator and its owner. We are invited at the same time to marvel at his generosity and abundant creativity and to recognise our accountability. Verse 2 is a picture we can't use as it stands. Thanks to satellites and all that we picture our world as a beautiful blue ball floating in the vast darkness of space. They pictured the world as a flat plate standing on pillars set in a huge sea and covered with a pyrex pudding bowl which kept the waters above the earth from deluging it. For them that picture conveyed a wealth of meaning. The waters and sea spoke of sheer power and surging danger and symbolised the reality and force of that great and life-threatening negative - chaos, with its minions of death, evil and sin. Hence the significance of "no more sea" in John's vision of the coming of God's kingdom on earth in Revelation 21:1. This also means that the story of the stilling of the storm is not just about disciples being saved from drowning and that those stories about crossing rivers are not just about getting to the other side.

The Old Testament contains at least four creation pictures: the familiar one following an ordered seven-day plan in Genesis 1:1-2:4a, an agricultural one exposing the ambiguities of life in the real world in Genesis 2:4b-3:24, a God versus the chaos monster one in Psalms 74:12-17 and 89:5-18 and Isaiah 51:9-11 (also Job 7:12, 26:12, 38:8-11) and a Wisdom one in Proverbs 8:22-31 and Job 28:20-28; all of which are brought into play in the Creation Hymn, Psalm 104. Verse 2 is another glimpse of the third of these. God is the King of Creation. He has defeated chaos and established order. He now rules the world.

Verses 3-6 contain a question, an answer, a promise and a declaration. The answer most Methodists would give to the question in verse 3 is "All who want to", for we belong to a tradition which believes that God's love is for all and his welcome is to all. The psalm seems to give a different answer, that only those who meet certain standards can join the celebration. The difference is more apparent than real, for we too believe that God's love changes things, or at least changes us. We belong to a tradition which recognises that belief and behaviour go together. We expect those who come to worship to be changed by coming. There is no doubt that God accepts us as we are. There is equally no doubt that that is not how he wants us to stay. Verses 4-6 speak plainly of what God expects of us and of what his love can make of us.

The mysterious little word *Selah* may originally have referred to some sort of liturgical action, maybe a festal shout or a pause for everyone to prostrate themselves on the ground. We don't know. An untranslated Hebrew word like this simply indicates that the translators haven't a clue what it means.

The procession arrives at the Temple and the leader demands that the gates be opened (verse 7). The gatekeeper demands to know who wants to be let in. He is told that it is the LORD, the "glorious king". This is the God who has proved his power in saving his people in the past. This "Lord of battles, God of armies" picture is not really to our taste, but this psalm comes from a culture where the battle between good and evil, light and dark, life and death was real enough to make this a living metaphor. The leader repeats his demand and the gatekeeper repeats his question. The leader's answer rounds off the psalm with a shout of praise.

The title "LORD of Hosts" is an ancient one. NJB has "Yahweh Sabaoth" which reminds us of the "Lord God of Sabaoth" in the old version of the Te Deum. The hosts in question are probably the heavenly host of sun, moon and stars though the armies of Israel is a possibility. NIV follows the Septuagint and translates the phrase by "the LORD Almighty". Although "Almighty God" was probably until recently the commonest term we used in addressing God, it has no direct literal equivalent in the Bible at all and taken literally is a dangerous idea indeed.

So the procession with the Ark enters the Temple. There God's kingly rule is proclaimed and celebrated. There they worship the "King all glorious above". There his people are equipped, encouraged and enabled to go out and live and work to his praise and glory, so that his kingdom may come and his will be done on earth as it is in heaven.

PSALM 42

Remembering God

Number three in my Desert Island list of books about the Old Testament is *The Courage to Doubt* by Robert Davidson, published by SCM in 1983 and still available. It looks at those parts of the Old Testament which cry out to God in anguish, asking Why? or How long? or Where are you? as well as those which voice doubts about his existence, his love or his ability to do anything about anything. It is a profound and pastoral book. Its first chapter is called *Worship and Questioning* and among other things deals with the Psalms of Lament.

Roughly speaking there are two sorts of psalms - Praises and Laments. In the Laments either individuals or whole communities cry out to God for help. The circumstances in which they were composed vary and many are no doubt stylised, but all share a sense of urgency and desperation. They are not afraid to ask the question - Where is God?

Psalm 42 is a Psalm of Lament, one of the individual ones, written in the first person singular so that each worshipper can use it to speak of their personal need. It divides into two parts and has a chorus (verses 5 and 11). Psalm 43 might originally have been its third part for it has the same chorus.

In the first part (verses 1-4) the psalm voices a double crisis. The first is that God is not there any more. Like a deer in a desert desperate for water the Psalmist thirsts for God - but to no avail. His tears are his only drink. And it has been like this for a long time. The second is that this is public knowledge. Others know about his despair. His friends are worried about him and keep asking how this can be. They know how important his faith is to him. And he himself doesn't need reminding about how active he was in the life of the church.

The second part (verses 6-10) is much more complicated. It is a mixture of hope and despair. It begins by restating the problem. "My soul is cast down within me". This is immediately followed by "therefore", which suggests that the way through this valley of shadow is to "remember" God. Unfortunately there are two problems here. The one is that in verse 6 we can't be sure what the allusions to "the land of Jordan" and Hermon mean and we know nothing about Mt Mizar at all. The other is that verse 8 is extremely hard to understand and may have got corrupted somewhere along the line. None the less, the psalm suggests that the way of coping with despondency is to "remember" God. This doesn't mean redoubling our efforts to pray in an attempt to feel the presence of God again, and I suspect that our sort of Christianity has dangerously over-emphasised that kind of religious experience. It does mean calling to mind what we believe about God; reminding ourselves of the old, old story.

So the psalm gives those reminders. Remember Mt Hermon and how it speaks of the grandeur of creation! Remember the Jordan river and how the People of Israel crossed it to enter the Promised Land! Verses 6-8 suggest that all who know this experience of God's absence should call to mind those two pillars of Old Testament religion - creation and redemption. The pictures of waves and floods in verse 7 remind us of how God subdued the waters of chaos to create order and life (Psalms 74:12-17 and 89:8-12) and how he brought his people safely through the waters of the Reed Sea and the Jordan to new life in a new land (Isaiah 51:9-11). Day and night are creation reminders too. This leads to the key word - "steadfast love" - God's utterly reliable, consistent and ultimately victorious kindness.

But then despair floods back in, the same old despair of the first part. You talk about remembering God, the psalmist says, but God has forgotten me! And to make things worse, his enemies add to his suffering by pouring scorn on him and his God. What is new here is that he mentions his actual suffering, possibly illness or persecution. The "enemy", death, is oppressing him. And still the question, Why?, goes unanswered.

Finally the chorus. It might signal the beginning of a return of confidence, the first streaks of a new dawn of faith. It might be a stoic refusal to give in to despair. It might be a commonsense recognition that these things happen, that these times come and so they will also go. It might be a recognition that the psalmist's feelings are not the last word. All that and more. But is it a challenge to the psalmist to "lighten-up", snap out of it and get a grip? Some Christians say that sort of thing to people who feel like the psalmist. I think not. I see the first two lines as a powerful restatement of his predicament: Why, O why, am I like this: empty, confused, in such a mess? And then, when that is faced up to and accepted, the psalmist is in a position to glimpse a "hope", a possibility of a future - notice that little word "again" sneaking in - in which the words "help" and "God" can be used in the same sentence.

And what is it that opens up this possibility of hope? Is it partly that the Psalmist has dared, even in worship, to speak what he feels, to admit that he is angry at God? And is it partly that the Psalmist is, even as he voices his despair of God, beginning to "remember" God?

PSALM 51

Repentance and renewal

Psalm 51 is the best known of the seven Penitential Psalms in the Psalter. We know nothing of its author or date of composition. The editor of the hymn book puts it on the lips of David "when the prophet Nathan came to him, after he had gone in to Bathsheba". That sordid episode can be read in 2 Samuel 11:1-12:13. We tend to think of it as David's adultery with Bathsheba, but Nathan's main complaint against his king was over his murder of Uriah. Incidentally, those who get anxious over the "establishment" of the Church of England might reflect on the fact that Nathan was the court prophet of the established church, which gave him a platform to address the king and the nation and to be heard.

According to the editor, Psalm 51 is a serious psalm of repentance and renewal after serious sin and crime. It begins by voicing a direct appeal to God - "Have mercy" in most translations but "Help me" is better. It can voice this appeal because the psalmist knows that God's name and nature is love - eternally reliable and abundantly generous kindness (verse 1). See the motto verse Exodus 34:6-7 which re-echoes throughout the Old Testament.

The psalm continues by acknowledging the past, verses 3-5. We should not be misled here. This is urgent and vivid language expressing the sinner's abhorrence of what he has done. It is the language of remorse rather than repentance (that comes later) and it is dramatically over-stated in the way the Bible does. It should not be used to create doctrines of "original sin", "total depravity" or the evil of sex. That is making the mistake of taking metaphorical language literally and hardening poetry into prose.

Next, in metaphor piled on metaphor, comes a plea for a new start. The sinner asks to be "washed" (verse 7, picking up from verse 2), made new (verse 10) and "delivered" (verse 14). He wants the past put behind him (verse 9). He wants to learn better ways (verses 6 and 12). He wants to "make a life of praise" (verses 14-15) to use that lovely phrase from *Hymns and Psalms* 474. The plea climaxes in verse 17. All that is necessary to receive God's forgiveness and its renewing and transforming vitality is repentance - "a broken and contrite heart". This is not about feelings or emotions, about crying and despairing. What Hebrew means by "a broken and contrite heart" is what we mean in English by an admission that wrong has been done and a serious intention made to turn away from it and set off in a new direction. Sacrifice is a difficult area for us - we'll look at it in our study of Psalm 103. Psalm 51 insists that repentance is only possible with God's help. It insists even more insistently that his help is readily given.

The psalm ends very oddly. Up to verse 17 it has been an individual penitential psalm but the last two verses go off at a tangent into an appeal for the rebuilding of the walls of Jerusalem. Is this just bad editing? No. The editor knows that wrongdoing has consequences and that these consequences can go way beyond the original wrongdoer. He saw that in the story of David. There was, however, a bigger example. Half of the Old Testament was written to explain the catastrophe of the destruction of Jerusalem in 597 and 586 BC. The explanation was a simple one, that the destruction and exile was a consequence of their wrongdoing. By adding these last two verses the editor makes the same point. Then he goes on to offer hope for the future. Once wrongdoing is admitted a new start can be made.

Psalm 51 is a serious psalm of repentance and renewal after serious sin and crime. It can be used both by individuals and by communities. But how and when should it be used? It is not for everyday use. More than that, I submit that most prayers of confession are not for everyday use either. Our official line is that there must be a prayer of confession in every service. And I question that. I remember one of my ministerial students in Ghana asking why we had prayers of confession in college prayers every morning and evening when they were so busy with college work in between that they didn't have time to sin! That's a good question.

Look at verses 10-12. They assume that normally your average Israelite had a clean heart, a right, holy and willing spirit and lived in God's presence enjoying the joy of God's salvation. I'm sure the psalmist didn't mean that they were wonderfully godly and terribly good or anything like that, but that they were human and that their ordinary everyday humanity was not "sinful". It might not be perfect, but it wasn't bad. I wonder what he would have thought about using his psalm for everyday or every week occasions? Might he have thought that confessing our sin every day in every prayer and every week in every service was a bit over the top? Might he also have thought that it devalued our God-given humanity and cast doubt on the grace of God at work in those who believe, to say nothing of the fact that it also trivialised sin? I suspect he would.

He did know, however, that serious wrongdoing was seriously wrong, and that it could and did destroy life's normal equilibrium. He knew that when that happened it needed to be put right, and by God's grace it could be. He had written Psalm 51 for just such occasions.

PSALM 82

A challenge to get the priorities right

Psalm 82 is one of those psalms which doesn't appear for use in worship in *Hymns and Psalms*. It's easy to see why not. It pictures a meeting of the Board of Directors of Earth plc. There is serious business on the agenda. The God who is chairing the meeting has to take the junior partners to task for failing in their duties. There are sackings ahead.

There are glimpses of a Heavenly Court in the Old Testament (Isaiah 6, 1 Kings 22:19, Job 1:6 and 2:1 and teasingly in Genesis 1:26) and there are those wonderful pictures of angels, archangels and all the company of heaven in the New: but despite Psalm 58:1 there is nothing like Psalm 82.

In Psalm 82 each nation has its own god or gods (you can see a fascinating trace of that idea in Deuteronomy 4:19, 29:26 and 32:8) and the Most High is supreme over them all. All the nations belong to him (verse 8). He delegates responsibility for their care and maintenance to his "sons". In this psalm the Most High is simply called "God" and in most of our translations his divine underlings are called "gods". NIV is unique in putting that word in inverted commas and there is no justification for doing it at all. You can see how it was interpreted at the time of Jesus by looking at John 10:34-35, and that too is a long way from its original and literal sense. There is no mention in this psalm of the LORD (Yahweh), the God of Israel, and no claim that he is the supreme God, let alone the Only One - all that was a late development in Israel's history. Many commentators say that originally the psalm began by saying, "The LORD (Yahweh) has taken his seat ..." and that an editor changed it to the more general, "God", but changing it that way round is hard to credit and there is not a shred of evidence to support it. Why don't commentators comment on what is there, rather than on what they would like to be there?

What have these gods done wrong that makes God threaten to banish and destroy them? Quite simply, they have failed to be proper gods. The job of a proper god is to maintain justice; and they have not done that. The result is that the whole creation is hovering on the verge of chaos, its very foundations shaking (verse 5). It is the responsibility of gods to promote justice and to be defenders of the weak. And that is what they have failed to do. Does this lie behind the comment by Eliphaz in Job 4:18? Defending the weak is also the responsibility of kings and rulers, the representatives of the gods on earth, as Psalm 72 and Isaiah 11:3-4 make equally clear. This is radical stuff. The mark of a true god or a true king is not power and authority, but power used in care for the weak and needy. Failure to do that means that these gods should suffer the death penalty. The idea of gods dying is absurd, but what a powerful way of jerking everyone awake and getting them to grasp the enormity of the issue!

You will find no clearer picture of what the Old Testament means by justice than in verses 3-4. It is rather different from our idea of justice as an ideal and an abstraction, which judges serve by acting with total impartiality to ensure that its scales are always perfectly balanced. It is to do with actively promoting the interests of the marginal and displaced so that everyone has a stake in society and a life worth living. A judge must put things right, sort everything out and remake the wholeness and harmony that there should be. A judge must right wrongs, lift up the fallen and stop those who knocked them down from doing it again. That, the Most High says in accusation of these gods, is what they have failed to do. The psalmist - or should we call him a political commentator or a prophet? - sees that these failed gods are condemned and shouts out that the Most High himself must now set about doing what they had failed to do (verse 8). He prays that God will "save" the world, which gets the sense of the Hebrew over much better than "judge", a word which has so many negative overtones for Christian readers.

I cannot imagine the sort of Temple liturgy in which this psalm would have been used. Nor have I ever been in any service anywhere where this psalm has featured. Is it evidence for the existence of an Inter-Faith, Anti-Poverty, One-World service on Politics Sabbath in ancient Israel? There's a thought.

This odd psalm presents a challenge to our multi-faith, multi-cultural and multi-ethnic world. It presents one to churches and Christians who major on disputes over theological and ethical minutiae or detailed questions of liturgical correctness. Much like the saying in Matthew 23:23 or Micah 6:8 it is a call to get things in perspective and to get priorities right. What about adopting it as our Ecumenical Agenda for the Millennium? And I don't mean "ecumenical" in its narrow sense of Christians together but in its richer one of the togetherness of the whole inhabited earth? If we did that *Jubilee 2000* would be the first thing on our agenda and the very least we could do.

Psalm 82 suggests that the God of all faiths has made his will and purpose plain for all faiths, cultures and ethnicities to see and to do. Have we the ears to hear?

PSALM 100

Simple celebration of the shepherd

The *Jubilate* is a skylark song in spring. It's as bright and upbeat as it is short and simple.

The first two verses are a threefold call to *all the earth* to worship the LORD with *a joyful noise, gladness* and *singing*. There is a place in worship for quietness, more space than Methodists usually give it. There is a place for sadness and sorrow, the state of the world often demands it. But there is also a place for singing "happy songs" as the Good News Bible puts it. This example shows that happy songs don't need to be trite.

Verse 3 reminds us about how and where worship begins. It begins in *knowing that the LORD is God*. It begins when we acknowledge that God *is*. I will use that word, acknowledge, again and again because it is key to this psalm. In this verse we are invited to acknowledge that we owe our existence in every way to God. We are made by him and looked after by him. I know this rural picture is one that townies complain about. I also know that country folk are very aware of the fact that most sheep exist to be turned into lamb chops. So any offers to improve on this metaphor will be gratefully received, though I don't think you'll succeed.

If worship begins when we acknowledge that God is and that he matters, it continues as we experience his presence. You can't improve on Archbishop William Temple,

> *"Worship is the submission of all our nature to God.*
> *It is the quickening of conscience by his holiness;*
> > *the nourishment of mind with his truth;*
> > *the purifying of the imagination by his beauty;*
> > *the opening of the heart to his love;*
> > *the surrender of will to his purpose -*
> *and all of this gathered up in adoration, the most selfless emotion of which our nature is capable and therefore the chief remedy of that self-centredness which is our original sin and the source of all actual sin".*

There is an ancient translation problem in the second line of this verse. In the text of the Hebrew Bible it has "It is he that made us, not we ourselves" as in the AV. All the modern translations follow an ancient alternative from the margin of the Hebrew Bible - "and we are his." They are almost certainly right to do this, but the wrong reading is a good one for putting us in our place when we get too uppity and over-confident.

We know that God can be found always and everywhere. The Old Testament, however, is reluctant to say that he can be worshipped at any time and in any place. That reluctance is wise. "Always", "anytime", "anywhere" and "everywhere" are slippery words. Remember that Church Council which decided that something or another was everybody's job? Did it get done? Of course not. If it's everybody's job then nobody does it. Humans are like that. That's why we need special times and special places. So in verse we enter the Temple, the special place, for a service.

But this psalm does not talk about worshipping God. It talks about worshipping the LORD. It is a psalm which acknowledges that the LORD is God. There were other gods on offer, other names to honour, others who might be worshipped in the Temple. This psalm insists that it is important to get your god right. That is what the phrase "Bless his name" means. Some modern translations seem to think that "bless the LORD", "praise the LORD" and "thank the LORD" all mean the same. They don't. To bless the LORD, or bless his name, is to acknowledge that the LORD is the only God for Israel. It is to acknowledge that he is the one who is the shepherd of Israel, who rescued his flock from Egypt, guided them through the desert, brought them into the rich pasture of the promised land and who looks after them now. Of course Israel is thankful to him for that and much else besides. Of course Israel praises him for it, declaring what he has done. But above all Israel names him as the one who has done it and commits herself to honour him alone. She "acknowledges that the LORD is God". That is what it means to "bless the LORD". It is to say, as the crowds did to Elijah on Mt Carmel, "The LORD, he is God! The LORD, he is God!" (1 Kings 18:39). So to respond to the invitation, "Let us bless the Lord" with "Thanks be to God" is too feeble by half. Sadly we are centuries too late to change it now.

In verse 5 we come to the heart of the psalm. It is a snatch from a mini-creed which crops up throughout the Old Testament. Exodus 34:6-7 is the key passage. Among its echoes are Numbers 14:18, Psalms 86:15, 103:8, 111:4 and 145:8, Joel 2:13, Jonah 4:2, Nahum 1:3, Lamentations 3:21-24, Nehemiah 9:17 and 2 Chronicles 30:9. These verses come from different strands of Old Testament literature and thought, and from writings which are, as far as we can tell, from very different periods and ages. If you asked an ancient Israelite, What is your God like? then she would have pointed to the exodus and said, "That is what he is like, a God who sets us free." If she was pressed further it looks as if she would go on to say, "The LORD is good: his steadfast love endures for ever, and his faithfulness to all generations." We will explore this more fully when we read the magnificent Psalm 103.

PSALM 103

Ancient hymn for a desert island

Psalm 103 is my desert-island psalm. If I was allowed only one chapter from the Old Testament this would be it. If I was allowed only two chapters from the whole Bible this would be one of them. This ancient hymn is, to this reader at least, a summary of everything that is best in the whole Bible, not just the Old Testament. Almost everything that needs to be said about God is here. The only bit missing is that everything said here is lived out in Jesus of Nazareth.

The psalm begins and ends on that note of "blessing the LORD" which we saw in Psalm 100. It begins with the acknowledgement that of all the gods on offer it is the LORD alone who is God and who is the source of life and blessing (verses 1-4). It ends with a call to the whole universe to give the LORD the acknowledgement which is his due. In fact, the psalm begins and ends in much the same way that the Lord's Prayer begins and ends. The only difference is that in the first and last words of the psalm everyone who sings or prays the psalm is invited to make that acknowledgement their own - "Bless the LORD, my soul".

The kernel of the psalm, verses 6-18, is an expanded commentary on that mini-creed which cropped up in Psalm 100:5 and of which Exodus 34:6-7 is the key passage. The great words are *steadfast love* (verses 4, 8, 11 and 17) and *mercy* (verses 4, 8 and twice in 13) with *righteousness* (verses 6 and 17) and *justice* (verse 6) not far behind. These are lovely, warm words. They speak of a love which will not let us go but which seeks us out with kindness and embraces us with generosity. They speak of a new-every-morning sort of love, which takes our sins, our mistakes and all the sad and sorry failures of our lives and puts them behind us. *Righteousness*, in this psalm and in the Old Testament generally, means a love which yearns and works to put things right. *Justice*, likewise, is love in action to restore things to how they ought to be. So, crucially, when the Old Testament describes God as our *judge* it doesn't picture him as the impartial and unbending judge of a Roman court but as the one who springs to our aid to sort everything out and make it right again. Confuse the meaning of the Hebrew word with the meaning of the Latin one, as much theology does, and you get things seriously wrong. Stay with these verses in this psalm and you'll avoid that pitfall.

Distinctions between these words can't be drawn too rigidly. We see that from the way the different terms are used in parallel to each other (eg *righteousness* and *justice* in verse 6 and *righteousness* and *steadfast love* in verse 17). Added together, they paint a picture of a God who is generously kind and utterly reliable. They point to our "Covenant God" who wants to be involved with us and who stays by us despite our failings. Anyone wanting an alternative Old Testament reading for the Covenant Service can find one here. Another is Exodus 34:6-7 in the NRSV. This translation follows ancient Jewish tradition in reading "thousands of generations" rather than simply "thousands", and in so doing opens up the meaning of the passage much better. It emphasises God's amazing generosity in a typically Jewish and over the top way: his love lasts for thousands of generations, his anger for a mere three or four.

Those who have problems with the picture of God getting angry at all need to stop for a moment and think about it. The clue to understanding God's anger is found in verse 13 which pictures God as a father. We wouldn't think much of a parent who didn't get angry when their children fouled up their own lives or the lives of other people, would we? We might even say that anger, frustration and the tears in which they show themselves are a mark of love. In the Old Testament, God's anger is a sign that he actually cares. And we wouldn't think much of a parent who didn't get angry when someone else was hurting their child, would we? In the Old Testament, God's anger is sometimes the only defence the weak and helpless have against the strong and vicious.

Some Christian theology, on the other hand, has taught us that God's anger is his normal emotion towards us. We are sinners and we deserve it. We have offended against God's justice and so he has no alternative but to be angry and punish us. This is becoming the standard presentation of the death of Christ in much modern preaching and evangelism. Jesus had to die to pay the price for our sins and he died as a substitute for us to satisfy the demands of God's justice. Am I wrong to think that verses 10-14 of this psalm show that all of that theory is at best unnecessary and at worst misguided or even pernicious?

These verses must not be read as if they minimise sin or deny its horrible effects. They take sin seriously. But they also show how God deals with it. How? He forgives it. Why? Because he's like that. And if that's what normal and loving parents do, can you really expect God to do or to be anything less (see Matthew 7:9-11)?

This is my Old Testament in a nutshell, desert island, psalm. It is simple, sane and humane. Thanks be to God for it.

PSALM 131

Humility is healthy

From the beginning Christianity has insisted that humility is a virtue. St Paul frequently taught his church members that they should be humble. In the gospels we see Jesus not only teaching about humility but also practicing what he taught. All of this was contrary to what was being taught in the Greek culture of the day. There humility was seen as a vice rather than a virtue. It was a sign of weakness. In their macho society you were expected to stand on your own feet, claim your rights and assert yourself. Jesus lived and taught a different message - that it was a gift to be humble. And if Jesus is a model of humility for us, then we also see that being humble is not about being Uriah Heapish nor about allowing yourself to be used as a doormat.

Where did Jesus get this radical idea from? An answer you still find in some Christian circles is that Jesus invented it and then Christianity promoted it. Not so. The right answer is that here, as in so many ways, Jesus was a good son of Abraham. He taught and lived out what he had learned from his Jewish faith. The roots of this idea of humility are found in the Old Testament (eg Numbers 12:3, Isaiah 66:2, Micah 6:8) and Psalm 131 is a little gem of a psalm where some of them are made beautifully clear.

In the first two verses the psalmist addresses God. He admits that once he was proud. Now, however, he has recognised that pride to be a sin and has found another way to be. His *heart* is no longer *lifted up*. For us *heart* is a metaphor for emotions and feelings; for the Old Testament it is a metaphor for the will. People whose hearts are lifted up have a driving ambition. They know where they are going and intend to get there. They set their own agenda and are ruthless in achieving it. Even their best friends would admit that they were pushy. Others would call them arrogant. The psalmist has turned away from all of that. He has come to the Gethsemane point where he can say, "Your will, not mine, be done". His *eyes* are not *raised too high*. The key to this is Isaiah 37:23. The Assyrians were notorious as a vicious and tyrannical enemy, marked by arrogance and pride (see Isaiah 10:12-15 and 37:21-29). The psalmist says that he no longer behaves like an Assyrian. Finally he admits that he has come to accept his limitations. There are things *too great and too marvellous* for him to understand. There was a time when he had talked freely and readily about such things: but now he knows when to speak and when to be silent. He has learned intellectual humility too.

The second verse paints a picture of this. He is like a three-year-old sitting contentedly on its mother's lap. He used to be like a two-year-old, demanding to be fed (they breast fed children much longer in those days) and throwing a tantrum if it didn't get enough attention. It has not been easy for the psalmist to reach this point. He has had to work on his soul - his passions, drives and needs - as hard as a farmer has to work to prepare the hard ground for sowing. That is the sense of the Hebrew word translated "calmed".

In the third verse the psalmist turns to address Israel. We know nothing of who wrote this psalm, when, where or why: but it certainly ends on a wider note than the personal with this appeal to Israel to *hope in the LORD*. Just as he had learned to do that rather than trusting in his own ability or enterprise or whatever, so he appeals to the nation to put their ambitions and grandiose plans aside. That is not what being the People of God is about. We can imagine particular circumstances in which little Israel was tempted to play the superpower game, though never with the remotest possibility of succeeding. We can also read elsewhere in the Old Testament about the ways in which the Chosen People celebrated their superiority. The psalmist will have none of that. Israel must, at the very least, put away aggressive, military and nationalist ambitions. The future does not lie that way.

Finally to the title. A *Song of Ascents* probably means a pilgrim song. Pilgrims can get carried away and their religion can get very triumphalistic. *Of David* shows a link with the monarchy. Rulers can get delusions of grandeur. Does this double title invite us to see this little psalm as an antidote to both sins?

Humility, in the Old Testament, is the opposite of pride. Pride puts self at the centre. Humility, in contrast, accepts that God is in the centre and challenges us to admit that we depend on him and to be willing to subject ourselves to him. Humility, secondly, recognises the value of other people and encourages us to pay them due regard and to be willing to give ourselves away in service to them. Thirdly, humility recognises our individuality, value and worth but invites us to make a realistic assessment of ourselves, our place and our potential. It is an ethic for individuals and for communities. You can see why it wasn't very popular with the ancient Greeks and why it isn't all that popular today either. Some even say that it is "unhealthy" and want to leave it out of our modern Christian ethic, much like *Hymns and Psalms* 538 has dropped out of our modern repertoire. That would be a mistake too.

PSALM 150

Praise the Lord

Psalm 150 is the last psalm in the *Book of Praises* of the old Jerusalem Temple and the last entry in *Hymns and Psalms*. Every verse in it begins with "Hallelu-" and ends with an exclamation mark. In its six short verses it has thirteen imperatives calling us to "Hallelujah!" It is, as my NRSV calls it, the Doxology marking the end of the Psalter and a fitting climax and conclusion to the book of Psalms.

Hallelujah became a full-throated Hebrew shout of praise, and it's much easier to say with the oomph it deserves than its anaemic Greek cousin *Alleluia*. *Hallelujah* was a shout of praise which became a popular and enthusiastic congregational response in Jewish worship when their new service book and new hymn book were introduced in the new Temple built after the Exile. The first Christians used it too. We see it in the great hymn sung by the angels and archangels and the whole company of heaven in Revelation 19:1-8 and it has featured in Christian liturgies ever since. "Praise the LORD" is our usual English translation and to shout *Hallelujah* or to "praise the LORD" is to express, joyfully and thankfully, our appreciation to God for what he is and what he has done. That is what Psalm 150 invites us to do.

If we ask, *Where is God to be praised?* verse 1 gives us two answers. The first and obvious one says "in his sanctuary". It speaks of the worship offered by God's people at those special times and in those special places which he has given to us. It points to worship as the first priority of church life and reminds us that the heart of worship is the praise of God. We know it's not always like that of course, but this verse reminds us that it should be. The second answer is even more challenging - "in his mighty firmament", that is, under his great pudding bowl of the sky. God is to be praised always and everywhere, by lives as well as lips, in the world as well as in the church and seven whole days not one in seven.

If we ask, *What is God to be praised for?* verse 2 gives us two answers: for what he does and for what he is. Some of us have problems with "for his mighty deeds" and what God does. It was popular in theological circles to talk about "a God who acts" until Auschwitz put an end to such talk. Some today talk about "signs and wonders" but most of us are uneasy because we can't help thinking about when good things don't happen. No doubt the psalmist would point to mighty deeds like the defeat of national enemies, but do we really believe that God fights battles and ensures that the right side wins? And when God's intervention in our lives is reduced to finding us parking spaces in busy streets then the whole idea seems inadequate let alone unworthy. Life and God don't seem to work like that. I think God's "mighty deeds" are something else, that he has the last word. After all, we are still here. Goodness, truth and justice have not been destroyed by evil, death and sin. Is not God's really mighty deed the continuing victory of life over death, good over evil and light over darkness? The second answer - "for his surpassing greatness" takes me straight back to the greatness of his love as in Psalm 103 and those key words in Exodus 34:6-7.

If we ask, *How is God to be praised?* verses 3-5 give us part of an answer. They invite us to praise God in our worship with music and dance. I make no comment here about old versus new except that whatever style of music we use in worship it has got to be good. *Hymns and Psalms* 377 says it all for me: but please excuse me from the dance bit.

If we ask, *Who is to praise God?* the answer in verse 6 is stunning. "Everything that breathes". Not just Jews but all humanity. Not just humanity but all that breathes. What a wonderful choir to be part of. This last psalm in the book invites the whole of creation to join in the praise of God.

So what is Psalm 150 asking of us? One or both of two things.

The word, *Hallelujah*, was probably first used as a call to worship said by a worship leader to a congregation. He would say, "Praise the LORD", and they would respond by saying or doing something. We can therefore hear this whole psalm as a call to "make a life of praise", to use that splendid phrase from *Hymns and Psalms* 474, and respond to that call by asking God to make it possible, as in that best of all hymns, 792.

Later on the word *Hallelujah* itself became a congregational response and a cultic shout, a one-word act of praise. We can say this psalm in that way, making it our act of praise. In these studies we have dipped into the Psalter and sung those hymns which speak of God's grace and glory and of his presence and his power. We have also sung those which plead for his help, urge his action and anguish over his absence. The Psalter ends all of this by giving us this psalm to sing, inviting us to say,

> "Through all the changing scenes of life,
>   in trouble and in joy,
> the praises of my God shall still
>   my heart and tongue employ."

Either way. Let it be so. Amen.

Isaiah 1-12

If the Book of Isaiah as we now have it is a symphony, containing many themes and developing them in many ways into a finished whole, chapters 1-12 are the first movement and chapter 1 is the overture in which all the themes are introduced. The symphony comes from an unknown composer who used the works of others, acknowledging a debt to one in particular in the title given to the finished work, "The Vision of Isaiah". In these studies we look at the "First Movement", sometimes taking an overview and sometimes concentrating on no more than a moment in the melody. This symphony is part of a wider collection. In the Hebrew Bible it is the first of four "Explanations" (Isaiah, Jeremiah, Ezekiel, The Twelve) which follow four symphonies which make up "The Tragedy" (Joshua, Judges, Samuel, Kings). The Tragedy is the story of the People of Israel from a bright beginning on the wrong side of the Jordan River into and then, after a series of sorry tales, out of the Promised Land and away to exile in Babylon. It ends with the tiniest glimmer of hope for a new future. The theme of all four "Explanations" is the same - the People of Israel are the People of God and the tragedy is that their misfortune is of their own making. They have brought it upon themselves by their disobedience and wrongdoing. If there is to be any future for them it will be by God's generosity in giving them a new start. That too is the theme of the First Movement of the Isaiah Symphony in Isaiah 1-12. The recording we listen to is that of the NRSV.

1   The time and the place - Isaiah 1:1-9

The Bible's title for the Isaiah Symphony is "The *Vision* of Isaiah". *"Vision"* immediately suggests a secret look at what is not really ours to see and an experience which is frightening and hopeful at the same time. It invites us to see things from God's perspective. It promises to reveal the real state of present affairs, to expose their causes and to show their consequences. We are invited to listen with both foreboding and excitement.

In verse 1 the vision is set in a particular time and place - Judah and Jerusalem from 742 to 701 or 687 BCE - and given to a particular person. These were years of international crisis. For much of the time Assyria dominated the region, exacting tribute, causing panic and wreaking havoc. The prosperous kingdom of Israel was destroyed in 722 with the fall of its capital, Samaria. The smaller kingdom of Judah struggled through, but was devastated after Hezekiah rebelled in 705. Jerusalem survived siege in 701 only because it surrendered. This is the historical situation which forms the scene for God's message through "Isaiah the son of Amoz". In it we see not only the national and international scene, but also the local and the personal in which ordinary people lived and died, prospered, suffered and survived, and we hear what God has to say about it.

In verses 2-9 we see the incomprehensible horror which is at the heart of Isaiah's vision. God calls on heaven and earth to witness the shame - his children have rebelled against him. Every attempt at correction has failed. They have brought terrible destruction upon themselves. In it all we feel God's pain, frustration and despair. Is there any future for his children and for Zion, his "daughter"?

2   Worship or blasphemy? - Read Isaiah 1:10-17

The second "Hear" of Isaiah's message is addressed to the national leaders in Jerusalem. This city is so far from what it should be that Isaiah calls it by the same name as the proverbially sinful city of "Sodom" and its twin, "Gomorrah". It is also, thanks to God's grace and nothing else, only fractionally away from sharing the same destruction (verse 9).

We have already seen that the nation is deeply if not mortally corrupt (verse 4). Despising their God they are estranged from him and from each other - these two relationships being indissolubly bound together in every strand of Old Testament thought - and the result is chaos. But as yet no one else is aware of the tragedy which Isaiah has been shown. Life is good. God is good. The religious life of the Temple is flourishing. But God sees it differently and rejects all of it (verses 11-15). These verses (akin to Amos 5:21-24, Hosea 6:6 and Micah 6:6-8) are not an attack on worship itself, but on that sort of spirituality which allows the rest of life to remain untouched by God's demands. Such religion is fatally flawed, and verse 15 says why with brutal simplicity. By contrast, true religion begins with listening to God's "teaching" (*torah*, verse 10) and continues by putting it into practice, negatively by "ceasing to do evil" and positively by "learning to do good" (verses 16-17). The mark of such practice is "justice" (*mishpat*) and its litmus-test is the care of the vulnerable.

3   God's anger - Isaiah 1:18-31

Having shown them in starkly simple terms what he requires (verses 16-17), God speaking through his spokesman now asks them pointedly if they are going to change their ways (verses 18-20). If they are, the past is forgiven; if not, they will reap what they have sown. This is classic Deuteronomic and Wisdom teaching that faithfulness is rewarded and sin punished and it runs through this whole section. Though it is a rather rough-and-ready, rule-of-thumb sort of doctrine, and protests against its shortcomings are found elsewhere in the Old Testament, yet is there not some truth in it?

Verses 21-23 take up again the picture of "daughter Zion", no longer virginal but prostituted, the victim of abuse by those in positions of power and responsibility. Note again how the treatment of the vulnerable ("the widow, the orphan and the poor" is the common Old Testament designation for them) is singled out as a marker at the end of verse 23. But Jerusalem is not yet beyond help. The process might be drastic ("smelting" verse 25), but by justice (*mishpat*) and righteousness (*tsedaqah*) it can be done (verse 27). These two great and warm Old Testament words, so often misunderstood by Christians, refer both to God's strenuous effort to put things right and keep them right arising out of his deep love for his people and to our living and working in the same spirit for the common good.

Verses 29-31 give us our first encounter with horticulture. Of that more later.

The overture ends with a vision of fire which no one can quench. In it there have been glimpses of hope, but are these only fleeting moments in an overall mood of gloom and doom? This question will be raised throughout the first movement and all through the Symphony. We have heard the theme rehearsed in the overture: the Holy One of Israel (see chapter 10 on p46 for this distinctive title for God) has a claim on his people, and they have failed or been failed by their rulers. The consequences are shared by ruler and people alike - chaos leading to destruction. But will it come to that? If God is in all of this, then out of it or after it might there be possibilities as yet undreamed of?

4   Swords into ploughshares - Isaiah 2:1-9

Verse 1. The overture is over and the first movement continues with a new heading about the "word" ("message", "matter" or "content") which Isaiah saw in his vision.

In verses 2-4 the prophet sees the first of those visions of hope and dreams the first of those dreams of peace which are such a moving and memorable feature of the Symphony. A day will come when people of all nations will listen to the teaching (*torah*, "instruction", verse 3) of Israel's God, and in living by it ("walking in his paths") will find harmony and fulfilment. Note again the positive sense of "judge" in verse 4, that "God will put all things right between the nations ..." Maybe all we can do after reading this is to pray, "Thy kingdom come ... " or to ask with the Psalmist, "How long, O Lord, how long?" A longer form of this vision is found with some detail differences in Micah 4:1-4.

Verses 5-6 are an invitation by the prophet to the people of Judah to walk with him "in the light of the LORD", using the metaphor of "walking" already seen in 2:3 and familiar especially in the Wisdom tradition with its contrasting "two ways" or "paths" (eg Proverbs 2). They are lost and the prophet offers to put them back on the right road.

But no sooner is that said than the prophet begins a sustained attack, taking what will prove to be a distinctive line. Instead of talking *to* his hearers ("you" in verse 6a) he distances himself from them and begins to talk *about* them in the third person ("they" in verse 6b). *They* are doomed! Why? Because of their pride!

The situation in Jerusalem is the reverse of what Isaiah had seen. Instead of foreigners coming to Jerusalem to learn of God they are welcomed as religious teachers (verse 6). Instead of beating swords to ploughshares they have multiplied their chariots (verse 7). Instead of recognising the true God they have created their own idols (verse 8). So instead of going up to the Temple they will be brought down to hide in caves and even in the dust (verse 10). Because they have exalted themselves they will be humbled. Verse 7a hints at the cause - pride comes with prosperity (compare Deuteronomy 6:10-12, 8:11-17, Hosea 13:4-6 and Proverbs 30:8-9).

5   Humbling the proud - Isaiah 2:10-21

If in verse 9 Isaiah expresses his revulsion at the level of degradation to which those who worship idols have sunk, though they of course are completely oblivious to it, in verses 10-21 he shouts them awake to the humiliation which is coming upon them which none of them can escape. They will be humiliated because of their pride.

There is of course a proper pride and an improper one, as there is a proper humility and an improper one. Isaiah is in no doubt that Jerusalem has exhibited the sort of "inordinate exaltation" which is Thomas Aquinas' definition of pride as a vice. There is also no doubt about the rigour of his condemnation in verses 10-19 of such self-confident attitudes and behaviour, piling on adjectives (haughty, proud, lofty, lifted up, high) and metaphors (cedars and oaks, mountains and hills, the latest technology of architecture or transport). Pride is condemned as that attitude which refuses to accept the sovereignty of God and which expresses itself in arrogant behaviour towards others and in an overweening opinion of one's own qualities or achievements. It is the abuse of power. It is anti-social in its outlook and destructive in its results.

All of this will be exposed "in that day" (verses 11, 17 and 20) when God "rises to terrify the earth" (verses 19 and 21) for the presumption that it is. Then the true majesty and glory (verses 10, 19 and 21) will be seen as God's and God's alone (verse 17). Here Isaiah uses traditional Day of the Lord and theophany language but like Amos (in 5:18-20) he gives it a violent twist: God's coming Day is *against* Jerusalem in its pride. Its terrors will indeed be experienced by God's enemies, but those enemies are his own proud people! That Day will also expose the idols these people cherish for the futility that they really are (verse 20). There is no reason for NRSV to translate the repeated phrase with "in that day" at 2:11 (and 3:18 and 4:1) but with "on that day" at 2:17 and 20 (and 3:7 and 4:2).

6   Misleading rulers - Isaiah 2:22-3:15

In verse 22 the prophet again speaks directly *to* his hearers and gives them advice. His advice is to recognise where real help and real power are to be found. When human beings get angry the most they can do is huff and puff, when God gets angry he can destroy as well as terrify. The wise person will therefore take notice of God.

3:1-8 is a strange passage. It talks of God taking the nation's leaders away - all the politicians, bureaucrats, lawyers, generals, scholars and priests. The result is anarchy and the suffering it brings (verse 5). This might be a reflection of what was actually taking place, leaders being exiled or those with the means to do so escaping to safety from a stricken city and leaving the rest in the lurch. Verse 8 points out that such chaos is a consequence of rebellion, which is pride.

In verses 9-11 the familiar reaping-what-you-sow theme recurs. The sarcasm of verse 12 prepares for the charge in court in verses 13-15, that "your leaders have mislead you". The courtroom drama is a popular device in the repertoire of the prophets (the best example is Micah 6:1-8). In Isaiah 1:1 God called on heaven and earth to be witnesses in his complaint against his people. In 1:18-20 he issued a challenge to his adversaries. Now in verses 13-15 he rises as Prosecutor and Judge to argue his case, and his accusation is the familiar one in other prophetic scores - Amos (2:6-7, 5:10-13, 8:4-6), Hosea (4:1-4) and Micah (2:1-2, 3:1-3, 9-12). The leaders will pay for their injustice. Note that the word "judge" in verse 13 is not the common and warm "judge" = "save" verb related to the noun in 1:27.

Guidelines to Isaiah 1:1 - 3:15

The naming of the kings in 1:1 alerts us to the fact that much of the vision will be to do with power - God's power and human misuse of power. It also exposes the folly of those who say that religion should be kept out of politics.

1:24 talks of an angry God. Some Christians jib at this idea. But is a God who doesn't get angry worth worshipping at all? There is much around us for a good God to get angry about! Isaiah believed that God got angry and took action. Many find it more difficult these days to think of God taking action in the way that Isaiah could, and ask how God can act in our world other than through his people. Does this mean that the Church should get a lot angrier than it does? Isaiah leaves us in no doubt what about.

The Vision of Peace in 2:2-5 is beautifully paraphrased in the hymn, "Behold the mountain of the Lord". The hymn by Lewis Hensley, "Thy Kingdom come, O God", combines prayer for the coming of that day with asking the Psalmist's question. Both hymns could usefully be used in your prayers or meditation.

The overture and what we have heard of the Symphony so far tells of threat and hope, "punishment" and "redemption", though more of the former in each case than the latter. Does this in fact speak to the realities of all times and all histories, ours included?

7   Contrasts - Isaiah 3:16-4:6

The mention of "grinding the face of the poor" (3:15) in the courtroom drama is followed in verses 16-17 by a return to the theme of pride. This time the accusation is made specifically against the women of Jerusalem, "the daughters of Zion", using a variation of the previous metaphors of "Daughter Zion" in 1:8 and the prostituted city in 1:21. Isaiah is not quite as crude as Amos in his condemnation of the female idle rich (Amos 4:1-3) but the point is the same. They are haughty, vain and promiscuous and they will get what is coming to them (compare verse 9). From verse 18 he spells out what they will suffer "in that day", and the loss of their fine wardrobes will be only the start. "In that day" the daughters of Jerusalem will suffer appallingly and so will Daughter Jerusalem (verse 26).

Then "in that day" this shame and degradation will be replaced with something really beautiful. There will be a new Jerusalem (verses 2-6). Verse 2 paints a picture of its rich agricultural prosperity. In verses 3-4 the picture is of the "holiness", that is the purity and moral goodness, of the washed and cleansed "remnant" who have been "selected to live" in the new Jerusalem after its purging by "judgement" (*mishpat*) and fire. Verse 4 might suggest that all the guilty have been cleansed (compare 1:18) but probably means that they have been eradicated (compare 1:20). The aim of God's "judgement" might be redemptive rather than punitive: but the prophets were in no doubt about what ought to happen to those who wouldn't see the error of their ways.

In verses 5-6 the picture is of God's blessing on the new Jerusalem. His newly rescued people will not follow a pillar of cloud and fire like their ancestors did, they will live safely under it. "Cloud" and "fire" are frequent metaphors for God's presence, most often for his terrifying power to destroy, but now he is present to protect and shelter. The prosperity, happiness and joy of the new Jerusalem is summed up in the word "glory" (*kabod*). Perhaps there is a hint in these verses that Jerusalem has now become the beacon pointing to God which the Vision of Peace dreamed for it?

8   The Song of the Vineyard - Isaiah 5:1-13

Something new happens at this point in the symphony. God sings a ballad to his loved one, though a song about an unproductive vineyard might not sound like much of a love-song. The ballad has the feel of a parable about it. It is very short and provocative. At the end God asks the audience for their verdict, but without waiting for an answer goes on to say what he will do to his useless vineyard (verses 5-6). The punchline comes in verse 7, and is reminiscent of the greatest Bible punchline of them all (2 Samuel 12:7). The defective vineyard is "the house of Israel" and "the people of Judah". So far "Judah" has always been paralleled by "Jerusalem", so finding these two together here might be significant.

Israel and Judah are the LORD's vineyard, and on them he had lavished every vinicultural care: but the result has been bad fruit. Two of the themes we have heard before are now back: exploitation (verses 7-10) and idle luxury and extravagance (verses 11-12). Verse 7 sums up God's disappointment with a play on words. He expected justice (*mishpat*) but got bloodshed (*mishpach*), hoped for righteousness (*tsedaqah*) but got cries of anguish (*tse'aqah*). Verse 13 has a timeless feel as it points out that the consequences of such living. Living as they do inevitably (note the "therefore" at the beginning of the verse, and again at the beginning of verse 14) brings death instead of life. In the future this might be exile, away from their land as the Assyrians exiled the people of Israel in 722 or into a wasteland of anarchy for Judah (compare 3:1-5). In the present, though they don't recognise it, they are already starved of that basic necessity of life - a sense of meaning ("knowledge").

9   Injustice and its rewards - Isaiah 5:14-30

This section spells out the threat of verse 13. The consequence of wrong living is death, "Sheol" (verse 14). The Old Testament knows the "kind and gentle death" of St Francis' hymn, but also death of another kind - greedy, voracious and devouring. The picture is of "Sheol", the underworld of the dead, like a giant octopus whose tentacles are always reaching out to grab victims and drag them down. In the Psalms, for example, we see illness or other forms of suffering as an individual being dragged down into the pit (eg Psalms 18:4-6 and 116:3-11). But Sheol, always trying to undermine and destroy life, attacks society too. Here the prophet uses this vivid metaphor to speak of the disintegration of society which he sees in his vision given by God. Note again the pride and humiliation language in verse 15 and the way that verse 16 insists that things are only right (justice and righteousness - *mishpat* and *tsedaqah*) when God is enthroned, exalted, in life and society, even if this means the destruction of those who make things wrong. Verse 17 is difficult in Hebrew and can be read either as a dismal picture of depopulation in which the ruins of Jerusalem are inhabited only by animals and foreigners or, preferably, as a picture of hope along the same lines as 11:6-9.

Verses 18-24 form a series of four "Woes", reminiscent of Amos 5-6, against the same target audience of the rich and powerful. ("Woe to ..." is better than NRSV's "Ah" here or "Alas" in Amos). These people are harnessed to evil like a horse and cart (verse 18), but they believe that God is on their side guaranteeing them victory and success. They are utterly mistaken. They have got things completely the wrong way way round (verse 20), just as Amos says. They have rejected God's *torah* (verse 24) and ignored his advice, and Amos says that of them too (2:4-5).

In verses 25-30 you can hear the din of battle and smell the smell of fear in a passage which is typical of so many in which we see the belief that God will punish his enemies by using other nations to attack and conquer them.

10   Isaiah's "call" - Isaiah 6:1-13

In chapters 6-8 we meet the messenger for the first time. Isaiah's name was mentioned at 1:1 and 2:1, but so far we have only heard the message that he "saw". Now we meet the man and his family. Chapter 6 seems an odd place to hear his testimony to his "call", as it's usually called, for we would expect to hear that at the beginning of a prophet's work, as we do with Jeremiah and Ezekiel. But here again the Book of Amos gives us something of a parallel. We don't meet the messenger there until chapter 7 when the priest Amaziah confronts him and demands an explanation. In Isaiah 1-5 we have been reading largely threat and denunciation after threat and denunciation. Is it now the time for an explanation? Who is this man? Can we trust his words? What sort of a prophet is this? Does this message have any credibility? These are the questions answered in the testimony.

Isaiah's testimony is about a vision in the Temple in 742. His words cannot describe what he felt but the outline is familiar to us. He saw God, enthroned on high as a King and attended by six-winged seraphs. He heard shouting or singing and God himself speaking. He smelt smoke and incense. He felt the building shake and he was terrified, ashamed and burned clean. It was an experience of the transcendent otherness of God, and it was awesome. In it he felt the "Woe" with which he had threatened others. But he also felt needed. He was confused but also commissioned. Yes, the message he had to give was indeed largely threat and denunciation. And no, nobody would take much notice. But in this testimony Isaiah tells us who he is, and where his message comes from (compare Amos 3:7-8 and 7:14-15).

The picture of God as King is not as common in the Old Testament as we might expect. It seems to have been part of the special theology of Jerusalem and the liturgy of the Temple, and we see it in such "Enthronement Psalms" as Psalms 93, 96, 97 and 99. The Isaiah Symphony's distinctive title for God is the "Holy One of Israel", a title used only four times outside the book but thirty-one times within it. The seraph's chorus, "Holy, Holy, Holy", focusses on God's holiness and celebrates it. To call God "holy", *qadosh*, is to acknowledge both his power and majesty and his love and purity, as Reginald Heber puts it in these words from his famous hymn,

> "Only Thou art holy, there is none beside Thee,
> perfect in power, in love and purity".

"Glory" means much the same thing. Isaiah, as in verses 3 and 5, also often calls God, "the LORD of hosts" (*YHWH Sebaoth*, "YHWH of hosts"), a title which was probably intended to honour him as the King of the Heavenly Host, that is, of the heavenly beings who surround his throne, or possibly of the stars or even of the armies of Israel. Much better to leave this ancient name with its possibilities open than to translate it as "the LORD Almighty" as is sometimes done.

Verses 9-12 are full of irony here and when they are quoted in Matthew 13:14-15. No doubt the irony reflects the experience of most of the prophets. Nobody takes any notice. The more they speak, the less anybody listens. If only people would listen it would be different, but they won't. The result is that the prophets see the worst of their fears come true. So verse 13 points out that at the very most there is only a tiny remnant left, a tree stump, cut off, separated, and we are left asking if these few good people are enough for a future?

11 A sign for a king - Isaiah 7:1-17

This chapter is narrative. In the story Syria and Israel (Ephraim) have formed a coalition against the rising power of Assyria and are pressurising Judah to join. King Ahaz panics. Isaiah goes to him with a simple message from God, "Don't worry about this threat. Ignore it and it will go away. Put your trust in God. If you don't he will give you something far more terrible to worry about than these two tiny nations, the full might of the Assyrians themselves!"

There is comedy in the detail, for example in Isaiah's contemptuous treatment of all the kings involved. "What are you worrying about?" he asks Ahaz. "Worrying about Syria? Syria is no more than Damascus its capital! Worrying about Damascus? It's no more than Rezin its king! Worrying about Rezin? He's nothing more than a "smouldering stump of a firebrand"! You are terrified of a devouring fire, but it's only a bit of charred smouldering stick!" Then again when Isaiah loses his temper. He invites Ahaz to ask for a sign, and suddenly Ahaz becomes the model of trusting faithfulness and comes out with the pious, "Far be it from me to ask the LORD for a sign". Isaiah, thoroughly irritated, says that he's getting a sign whether he likes it or not!

The sign itself is straightforward. Isaiah points to a young pregnant woman and says that by the time she has her son and he is old enough to tell right from wrong, then the threat from Pekah and Rezin will be long past. The Hebrew says simply, "the young woman has conceived and she will bear a son ..." Most recent translations get the tense right and NRSV and NJB also put in the definite article. The result is different from the traditional translations which are heavily dependent on Matthew 1:23 and its talk of a virgin birth. Although Isaiah's children were given distinctive names to reinforce his message (7:3 and 8:3) it is more likely that this woman is one of the king's wives and the name a "throne name" given to a royal child at birth (like those in 9:6) for "Emmanuel" ("God is with us") is mentioned again at 8:8 where he appears to be growing up to be king.

12   Signs and stumbles - Isaiah 7:18-8:15

This passage is difficult in places but essentially it is a commentary on the simple message of the previous chapter. In 7:18-25 four "In that day" threats clarify what will happen on God's Day of Action when he brings the Assyrians down on Judah, as he said he might (7:17). The first uses the language of plague, the second the vivid metaphor of "shaving", the third of depopulation when what few animals remain will be more than enough to feed the tiny population which survives and the fourth pictures fields reverting to wilderness.

8:1-4 gives a second "sign" involving birth and naming. The prophetess's son is named, "The spoil speeds, the prey hastens" emphasising that destruction is fast approaching. Before this child can say "Mummy" or "Daddy" Syria and Israel will be destroyed.

In 8:5-8 the threat is turned against Judah and pictured as a flood which the royal child of 7:14, now grown up, will see devastating his land. Or will he? Will the onlooking nations see Judah survive, with both the tiny threat of Israel and Syria and the huge one of Assyria coming to nought? That seems to be the sense of verses 9-10.

In the soliloquy of 8:11-15 we return to the simple choice God is offering Judah through Isaiah - trust him or come to dread him, expressed in a metaphor used in both Testaments - God is a stone which either offers protection or trips you up.

Guidelines to Isaiah 3:16 - 8:15

Most scholars regard 4:2-6 (and such verses as the last lines of 6:13 or 7:17) as coming from a later prophet than "Isaiah of Jerusalem", as they call the lyricist whose life and words form the basis of chapters 1-35 of the Book of Isaiah. They may well be right on both counts. But we are listening to a symphony in its final form, and the precise origins of some of the tunes are not of major concern. In the First Movement of the Isaiah Symphony the two parts of the reading in chapter 7, for example, form a vivid contrast and make good sense where they are - the gaudy and fragile finery of Jerusalem in the present set against the "solid joys and lasting treasure" of the Jerusalem to come.

Many times over Christmas you will have heard or sung that our Lord's birth "fulfilled" Isaiah's "prophecy", the point made in Matthew 1:23. But we have seen that the prophecy was not that sort of prediction, which means that Matthew has taken the verse out of context and made it mean something it does not mean in the story. He does the same in all the fulfilments of prophecy he quotes in chapters 1-2. At one level his use of Isaiah 7:14 is illegitimate, for the plain meaning of the Emmanuel sign is the one Ahaz understands. But at another level Matthew makes a valid point. In the story the sign is about salvation. Isaiah promises Ahaz that Jerusalem will be saved from Pekah and Rezin - and it was. Is Matthew using the old story and the old sign to say that a greater and fuller salvation is now here? Is he saying that though God's deliverence of Jerusalem in Ahaz's time was real enough, now in Jesus Christ we have something that makes that pale into insignificance? I think so. Matthew the theologian points us to "Jesus, *our* Emmanuel", in whom salvation is "fulfilled".

13   Glorious hope - Isaiah 8:16-9:7

Verses 8:16-9:1 conclude our Meeting with the Messenger which began at 6:1. We have heard him testify to his call, seen his encounter with King Ahaz and heard his message of doom and hope reiterated in different ways. In this parting speech he asks for his message to be kept safe by his "disciples", for everything he heard in his call has happened. He has spoken but few have listened. God is "hiding" from them (see 3:1-3) - for they cannot see his signs (verse 18) and are looking anywhere but in the right place for guidance (*torah*) (verses 19-22). So let it be. If they follow delusions they will be disillusioned. But then, for this is God's purpose through it all, they will be brought out of gloom into light (9:1).

"Disciples" may mean a formal group showing that Isaiah was head of a "school" of prophets, or it may simply refer to those who have taken him seriously. 9:1 alludes to events lost to us, but the meaning is plain. Isaiah signs off on a note of hope.

9:2-7 is another Vision of Peace (like 2:2-4, 4:2-6, 5:16-17) and another Isaiah reading used at Christmas. A new day is dawning, a day of light and joy, war and oppression are over, a new king comes to reign with God's power and blessing. This is sometimes called a "messianic" vision, which is an accurate description if we understand "messiah" in its original sense as "God's anointed", a title for the King of David's line in Jerusalem. Only after that dynasty was long extinct did hope for a future "messiah" emerge.

For the "Day of Midian" see Judges 7:15-25. Verse 6 might refer to the birth of a prince but probably refers to the accession of a king (see Psalm 2:7-9). The four names are "throne names" which express the hope placed in the new king and pray for its fulfilment. Some translate "Mighty God" as "Divine Warrior" or "Mighty Hero" (REB) but there is another reference to the king as God in Psalm 45:6. Whatever we make of these titles the passage clearly refers to a human king of David's dynasty. In the new reign of this Prince of Peace the land will enjoy harmony, prosperity and wholeness ("peace" - *shalom*) through his care (*mishpat* and *tsedaqah*). The Vision ends on a sharp note which we take up next.

14   Misfortune explained - Isaiah 9:8-21

In 9:7 the Vision of Peace ended on what I called a "sharp note", saying that the power behind the new peace is God's jealousy ("jealous love" - NJB) or "zeal" (see 37:32 and 63:15), a word which is translated as "fury" in 42:13 and 59:17. The "LORD of hosts" is the "jealous God" of the Second Commandment (Exodus 20:5). This divine love which wants the best for its loved one has all the force of passion, and is as dangerous as it is warm. This passage shows the violent savagery of such passion, and it does not make pleasant reading.

9:8-21 is an explanation of the destruction which has come upon the northern kingdom, Israel. It repeats the message we have heard constantly, that the consequence of living against God is destruction from him. As before arrogance and pride are cited (verses 9-10) as at the root of this attitude. As before foreign nations are cited as God's chosen agents to punish Israel (verses 11-12) though again the historical allusion here is lost to us. As before we read that people are culpable because they have not turned back to God (verse 13). As before the faults of national leaders are said to have put everyone in jeopardy (verses 14-16). As before we hear of the terrors of anarchy (verses 18-21).

But there is an angry relentlessness in these verses not heard before. Three times we read that God's "anger has not turned away" and that "his hand is stretched out still" (verses 12, 17, 21). Now he has no pity on any, not even on the innocent and the vulnerable (verse 17). We cannot take the easy way out and say that this passage speaks of the evil consequences that wrongdoing brings upon itself by some sort of cause and effect. Here God is pictured as active and responsible. He is the one who makes this happen.

At least we are left in no doubt about God's feelings.

15   No special treatment for Jerusalem - Isaiah 10:1-11

Having described and explained the suffering that has come upon Israel and its capital Samaria ("them" and "their" throughout 9:8-21) the prophet now addresses the listeners directly ("you" and "your"). In verses 1-4 he warns them that they will share the same fate, repeating in verse 4 the refrain used three times in chapter 9. We have met the complaints in verses 1-2 before. In verses 5-11 God speaks in the first person. Previously we have heard him speaking in this way only in the courtroom drama and the Song of the Vineyard. Now we hear him say that he is about to do what he threatened then (verse 6). But this announcement of "Woe" ("Ah" = "Woe") is as much a threat against Assyria as it is against Jerusalem. God intended to use the Assyrians to punish his own people who were so far away from him that he can call them a "godless nation", but in their arrogance the Assyrians went far beyond what he intended. They boast of their superiority (verse 8), their conquests (verse 9) and their future victory (verses 10-11).

You could be tempted to think that this reading only makes the bad impression of the one in the previous chapter worse. The God who announces that he was responsible for sending the Assyrians against Samaria admits that they were out of control! Yet there is another way of looking at it. Isaiah, together with the rest of the Bible, pictures God acting in history by manipulating nations and people to achieve his purposes. We see such a view clearly in Isaiah 10:6 or 45:1. At the same time Isaiah 10:16 also shows the shortcomings of such a belief, for the Assyrians do what they want to do rather than what God intends, which is exactly what Israel and Judah do most of the time. We can, of course, go for one or other of these two pictures and harden it into a doctrine: but the Old Testament does not do theology that way. For the Old Testament God is beyond doctrine and definition, so it paints pictures, tells stories and uses metaphors. Sometimes the result is dramatic and frightening, as in this passage and the previous one, but no less than some of the pictures in the parables of Jesus, and we don't read them literally or turn them into doctrines.

16   Or for Assyria - Isaiah 10:12-27

This passage contains two prose interruptions which act like points of emphasis in the music, and we will hear another one in the next reading. They are all no doubt later additions to Isaiah's original message, and it is easy enough to see when they were themselves composed and added: but we are listening to the finished symphony, and such questions belong elsewhere. Thus verse 12 interrupts the flow of Assyria's arrogant boasting and it puts God firmly back in control.

Verse 13a is an excellent nutshell description of pride.

Verses 15-19 announce that God will bring the boasting of Assyria to an end and destroy its power. Isaiah 36-39 (a duplication of 2 Kings 18:13-20:19) tells the story of the failure of the Assyrians at the siege of Jerusalem in 701, just when it looked as if they were at the height of their powers and on the verge of total success. Needless to say the Assyrian records which tell of their campaigns in Judah at this time don't tell the story in quite the same way. The picture in verse 15 holds pride up to ridicule, and the whole passage plays on the metaphor of timber.

The prose verses 20-27 take up the remnant theme from verse 19 but talk about the remnant of Israel and Judah. "A remnant will return" (verse 21) just as Isaiah had said when he called his first son by that name (7:3). "On that day" they will no longer be dependant on their conquerors but on their God (verse 20). But it will only be a chastened few, for though they had been like the sand of the sea they have been punished, for God's threat about putting things right even if it meant an end for wrongdoers was not an idle one (verses 22-23). Having been told who they really ought to fear, verses 24-27 reassure them about the Assyrian threat. The terrible destruction which the Assyrians were threatening (verses 10-11) will not take place. It is a burden and a yoke but no more, and in due course it will be removed. This should not cause them, nor us, to forget that God's threat of destruction is "decreed" (verse 22).

17   A new day is dawning - Isaiah 10:28-11:9

The dramatic poetry of verses 27b-32 marks the advance of the Assyrian army and the fear and flight it causes. They march to the very wall of Jerusalem and threaten it. In verse 33 the mood changes again and we return to the picture of 10:18-19. The forest of mighty trees will be chopped down, and in its place a little shoot will grow.

We first met Isaiah's horticultural interests in 1:29-31 and saw his use of "cedars of Lebanon" and "oaks of Bashan" as metaphors of arrogance in 2:13 and again in 10:17-19 and 33-34. There was also the "branch of the LORD" at 4:2 and the Song of the Vineyard in chapter 5. This is a different "branch" in 11:1 which in addition mentions shoots, a stump and roots (also at 11:10). There was a different "stump" at 6:13. Later on the term "Branch" become a title for the Messiah (Jeremiah 23:5, Zechariah 3:8) but it does not have that sense at 4:2 where the word is best translated as "plant" (REB) or "seedling" (NJB), not as "Branch" with a capital letter as in NIV, but it does have something of that sense at 11:1.

Verses 1-9 need little comment but much reflection and prayer. In 11:1-5 we have the picture of a new community or more likely its new leader. His qualities are spelled out but above all he is one who honours God (verse 3). Again we see that the care of the vulnerable is the test of true justice and the use of power. In verses 6-9 we see another vision of peace, a dream of the harmony and beauty of life when power is used rightly. The contrast with 10:27b-32 could not be more marked.

18   In praise of God - Isaiah 11:10-12:6

Verses 10-11 are the last prose section in the movement and repeat the "on that day" theme from the previous one (10:20). Verse 10 emphasises that all the world will look to the new messiah as 2:3-4 had dreamed, and verse 11 speaks of the remnant of the exiled and refugee Israelites being brought home. The first time that God "extended his hand" might be the Exodus or when he saved the local remnant, or it might be when he "stretched out" his hand in punishment (see 9:12 etc).

The poetry in verses 12-16 takes up the picture of returning exiles, and adds that the long hostility and suspicion between Israel and Judah will be ended. The note of hostility against traditional enemies in verse 14 is sad and reflects a certain ambiguity about the position of the nations who will flock to Jerusalem "in that day". The themes of crossing waters and making highways in verses 15-16 are not only exodus themes but also draw on the ancient story of the Battle against the Chaos Monster (see 51:9-11). They will cross the water by God's power, but this time it will be the Euphrates (= "the River") as well as the Red Sea. The highway through the desert is also taken up in 40:3-5.

Chapter 12 is the retrospect which brings the First Movement of the Isaiah Symphony to an end and contains two psalms of thanksgiving. In verses 1-2 the hearers are assured that "in that day" they will look back, recognise that God was rightly angry with them and be able to rejoice that now he has saved them (the word "conforted" is taken up again in 40:1). "In that day", when they have drunk from the wells of salvation (what a lovely phrase) they will sing praise to the God who has delivered them and testify to the watching nations of that deliverance (verses 4-6). Both of these short psalms echo the Song of Moses (Exodus 15) and a number of psalms, especially Psalm 118 (verse 2 quotes Exodus 15:2 and Psalm 118:14 and there are many other links), as well as many other places in Isaiah. Here and in Psalm 118 the restored and comforted Zion sings praise to God for her experience of salvation, and it is the "old, old story" which they sing (Exodus 15). However, the psalm which for me best summarises Isaiah 1-12 is Psalm 99. The parallel in plot, language and themes is quite remarkable.

Guidelines to Isaiah 8:16 - 12:6

Looking back on Isaiah 1-12 as a whole we can see it as a constant interweaving of the themes of threat and hope. These are the two possibilities which face us corporately, and our choices, individual and corporate, go a long way towards determining the outcome. But not all the way. Isaiah is ultimately optimistic, because he believes in the God he does, a God who is a saving God and whose will in the end will be done. In that perspective Isaiah's visions of peace are not daydreams.

Meditate on Psalm 99 and let it remind you of what you have read in these studies.

Now that we have listened to the First Movement of the Isaiah Symphony let me leave you with the words of one modern critic. At the end of a chapter on the prophets in *A Rabbi's Bible* (SCM Press 1991) Rabbi Jonathan Magonet says this,

> The prophet as the loyal opposition in our society is to be searched out, listened and responded to - provided we do not neglect at the same time to strengthen the authority and self-corrective powers of government and the discipline and self-purification of our religious traditions. But on another level, the prophet is also our dreamer of dreams who brings us the vision of what might yet be. To him or her we owe images of restoration and rebirth, of hope and reconciliation; of a humanity restored to unity, of the harmony of animal and human beings, and of a world without fear. These visions are always beyond the horizon, for the watchman on his tower can only see with growing dread the arrival of the foe. Without this vision we are condemned to a world without meaning or hope, but with it we might survive, yet again, the onslaught of our own self-mutilation.

The Bible Reading Fellowship

Guidelines to the Bible

The *Bible Reading Fellowship* serves Christians of all denominations worldwide. It exists to help people value, apply and share the message of the Bible, particularly through regular Bible reading and prayer. Christians in over 60 countries use BRF's Bible reading notes and growing range of resources for all ages.

The *Guidelines to the Bible* series contains running commentary on passages from the Bible with introductions and background information and is arranged in weekly units. Each week's material is usually broken up into at least six sections. You can take as much or as little at a time as you wish. The whole 'week' can be used at a sitting, or split up into convenient parts; this flexible arrangement allows for one section to be used each weekday. You will need a Bible to accompany the notes. The last section of each week is usually called 'Guidelines' and has points for thought, meditation and prayer. A short list of books, to help with further reading, appears at the end of most contributions.

Guidelines to the Bible aims to reflect current trends in the critical academic study of the Bible but in such a way that serious Christian readers will be stimulated to read the Bible regularly, and will be moved to thought, prayer and action. Contributors represent a broad range of contemporary Biblical scholarship.

Guidelines is published in three issues a year - January-April, May-August and September-December - at £2.70 per issue and is available from SPCK and all good religious bookshops.

Come back, Moses, we need you

Some notes on Exodus 34:5-7

from the author's Old Testament course
for the South West Ministry Training Course
and
the Department of Continuing and Adult Education
of the University of Exeter

      Many commentators call these verses a "formula" or a "confessional formula", for it seems to be something of a mini-creed which crops up in various places in the Old Testament and which echoes in many more. It also appears in one of the psalms of the Qumran Community (see the end of this chapter). The wording varies slightly from place to place. Exodus 34:6-7 is probably the oldest of them. The others are Numbers 14:18, Psalms 86:15, 103:8, 111:4 and 145:8, Joel 2:13, Jonah 4:2, Nahum 1:3, Nehemiah 9:17 (compare v31) and 2 Chronicles 30:9. These verses come from different strands of Old Testament literature and thought, and from writings which are, as far as we can tell, from very different periods and ages. We can probably conclude from this that this mini-creed said something important about God which was believed by most Israelites. We can surmise that if an Israelite from Old Testament times was asked, What is your God like? then the chances are that he or she would have pointed to the exodus and said, "That is what he is like, a God who sets us free." If they were pressed further it looks as if they might well go on to say, "The LORD is merciful and gracious, slow to anger and abounding in steadfast love." In fact the two go together. Exodus 34:6-7 is set in the exodus story and in most of the eleven places where this mini-creed is found there is a reference to the exodus nearby. This verse seems to be very near to the heart of what they understood about their God.

Exodus 34 is another version of the giving of the Law to Moses on Mt Sinai after they had escaped from Egypt. According to the story, when Moses had got down from meeting God on the top of Mt Sinai the first time, he found that the people had melted down their gold jewelry and were worshipping a Golden Calf. He had pleaded with God to forgive them, but then set about punishing them himself. In Exodus 34 Moses is back on the top of Mt Sinai again, and is given two new tablets of stone with God's law written on them to replace the original ones which he had thrown in sorrow or in anger at the people's folly. Then we read,

> The LORD descended in the cloud and stood with him there, and proclaimed the name, "The LORD." The LORD passed before him, and proclaimed,
>
>> "The LORD, the LORD,
>> a God merciful and gracious,
>> slow to anger,
>> and abounding in steadfast love and faithfulness,
>> keeping steadfast love for *the thousandth generation,*
>> forgiving iniquity and transgression and sin,
>> yet by no means clearing the guilty,
>> but visiting the iniquity of the parents
>> upon the children,
>> and the children's children to the third and fourth generation."

Apart from its rather obscure introduction - who is doing the proclaiming and to whom? - and one crucial other place, this is a straightforward passage to translate. What is given above is from the NRSV and I have put the difficulty in italics. The Hebrew simply says "for thousands" and NRSV (and GNB) follow the traditional Jewish understanding of the passage to mean "for thousands of generations". All the rest stay with the original wording.

An interesting question therefore is, which is the best translation here and at Exodus 20:6 where the same words and translations are also found? The letter or what Jewish tradition believes to be the spirit? Is Deuteronomy 7:9-11 a parallel?

God's loving goodness is the first thing mentioned about him in this ancient mini-creed, but when we read on these ideas are soon eclipsed by what follows. A God who "visits the iniquity of the parents on the children and the children's children down to the third and fourth generation" is not a God we warm to. Here all our stereotypes about the nasty God of the Old Testament come into play. But we should note carefully that this old saying in Exodus

34:6 puts God's "anger" in perspective, especially in the NRSV and GNB translations based on the traditional Jewish interpretation. His punishment might last for three or four generations, but his "blessing" lasts for a thousand generations! (Again see Exodus 20:6). The same point is made in a slightly different way in Psalm 30:5,

> "For his anger is but for a moment:
> his favour is for a lifetime.
> Weeping may linger for the night,
> but joy comes with the morning".

In Exodus 34:6 (repeated almost verbatim in Psalms 86:15 and 103:8) we have one of the most beautiful verses in the Old Testament, asserting that, "The LORD is merciful and gracious, slow to anger and abounding in steadfast love".

Three of these words are "ordinary language", commonplace, daily life sorts of words, but "steadfast love" is one of the Old Testament's great theological and ethical technical terms. "Steadfast love" translates the wonderfully warm and rich Hebrew word "*hesed*". The great wealth of meaning in this evocative word can be seen from the variety of ways it has been translated into English over the years: "mercy", "kindness", "loving-kindness", "steadfast love", "covenant devotion", "loyalty", "tenderness", "faithful love", "constant love" or just that overworked but basic, "love". There is a lot to be said for the NRSV's phrase, "steadfast love", for this captures an important aspect of God's love in the Old Testament where his love is often seen in terms of his covenant with Israel. God calls Israel to be his people, and pledges his loyalty and love to them in the covenant with Moses on Mt Sinai (Exodus 20-24, Deuteronomy 5). In response the people are obliged to honour God and obey him in all that they do. The Old Testament story tells of God's reliability, he keeps his promises and honours his covenant. His love is reliable, and this reliability is what is emphasised in the phrase used by NRSV, "*steadfast love*". NEB tries to put this across with "constant love" and NJB with "faithful love". GNB is hot on the reliability aspect with its "keeps his promises" but fails completely to make mention of the other aspect. In Psalm 103 the psalmist wants to honour, thank and praise God because he has experienced for himself the same continually faithful and loyal kindness, care and love which God has consistently shown towards the people of Israel. He testifies that God's feelings towards us are both lovingly warm and consistently reliable: unfortunately, as much of the Old Testament so frequently complains, ours towards him are often neither.

"Slow to anger" is ambiguous, as can be seen in the different translations offered. It is one thing to take the words literally and say that God is "slow to anger" but it is not quite the same to say that he is "long-suffering" or "patient" as we would say in more modern English. If we choose to say that God is patient, then we need to remember that there are limits to his patience. If we prefer to say that he is "slow to anger", then we need to note that he does get angry eventually. The reference here to God's anger is important. For all of his love and care expressed in the other words in this verses, God can become angry. Psalm 103:9 may be helpful here:

> "He will not always accuse, nor will he keep his anger for ever".

This verse fills out the meaning of the third phrase in Psalm 103:8 that God is "slow to anger", "slow to become angry" or "long-suffering". In the first line the psalmist uses a word from the law court which means to "have a controversy with" someone or to "have a complaint against" them. "Accuse" is used by the NRSV, REB and NIV, and is much better than the "chide" of the older versions. Mowvley puts it plainly in his commentary, "He does not prosecute his case against us for ever." In the second line there is a verb for "guarding" or "keeping watch" but no noun to say what is kept watch on or over. All the translations agree that the verb is talking about God holding on to or maintaining his anger, and to "keep his anger" means to harbour or nurse it, to remain angry or to let this anger grow. It is just possible that the line should be translated as "nor will he keep us prisoner for ever", which makes a good parallel to the first line. If the traditional translation is kept both lines stress the fact that God does not accuse people or remain angry for long. The psalmist has no doubt that God gets angry with his people, but at this point in his psalm he wants to emphasise the "not always" and the "not for ever". We tend to notice the references to God's anger, but that is not the main point that is being made. In my view NJB gives a poor translation of this verse, but it does get this emphasis right,

> "His indignation does not last for ever,
>   nor his resentment remain for all time".

God's anger is real, but he is "slow" to get angry, and his anger does not last long.

This is not, however, the impression that many Christians have of the God of the Old Testament. Neither do they normally think of that God as a God of love, as he is so warmly spoken of in Psalm 103:8. The prevalent idea of the God of the Old Testament among Christians is that he is, at best, a remote and powerful creator, and at worst a stern and forbidding lawgiver, who can be violent if not cruel. He is a God to be "feared" (as in Psalm 103:11, 13 and 17) and who makes rigorous demands upon his people (as in Psalm 103:18 and 20-21). There is certainly some truth in this picture of the God of Old Testament: but what Christians are not so quick to notice is that much of this picture can be found in the New Testament as well. It is simply not true to think that the Old Testament talks about a God of anger while the New Testament talks about a God of love. It is not right to put a divide between the Testaments like that, for both contain some very harsh pictures of God, and both talk about a God of love. It is not as if the Old Testament presents a nasty God and the New Testament presents a nice one. Both can picture God in ways that we find attractive, and both can picture him in ways we find frightening and disturbing.

Pictures of God's anger in the Old Testament must include the Flood in Genesis 6-8, where God decides to wipe all living things off the face of the earth and start again with Noah and the creatures in the Ark because everything had got so bad. In the stories of the exodus we shudder at the ten plagues inflicted on the Egyptians, and then at the ways God punishes the Israelites in the desert, not only for worshipping the Golden Calf but for other much less serious reasons as well. Later on there is the way that he lets his tribes be attacked or invaded because he is angry at them, and ultimately that he lets the Assyrians destroy the Northern kingdom and the Babylonians the Southern one a hundred and fifty years later. There are also examples of God's anger at particular individuals. Perhaps the one that sums up all my misgivings best is the story of God's anger at poor Uzzah, who was only trying to help. After he had captured Jerusalem and as part of his plan to make it into his capital city, King David decided to bring the ark of God into the city. The ark was being carried on a new cart pulled by oxen,

> "When they came to the threshing floor of Nacon, Uzzah reached out his hand to the ark of God and took hold of it, for the oxen shook it. The anger of the LORD was kindled against Uzzah; and God struck him there because he reached out his hand to the ark; and he died there beside the ark of God. David was angry because the LORD had burst forth with an outburst upon Uzzah..."   (2 Samuel 6:6-8)

At least David comes out of this story with some credit. God gets angry at people, but in the Old Testament there is also no shortage of people who get angry at him, and who say so, sometimes expressing their anger in worship as we can see in some of the psalms (eg Psalms 44, 74, 13, 109).

The New Testament equivalent of the story of Uzzah might be the statement in Hebrews 10:31, that "It is a fearful thing to fall into the hands of the living God".

Both the story of Uzzah and this verse from Hebrews speak a strange language to most of us today. They seem to belong to a world very different from ours, and almost speak of magic and the occult. For them the sacred world is full of mystery and even terror. God is to be approached only through the proper channels, by the proper people in the proper ways, and anyone else who comes unprotected into the presence of the power and force of God is greatly at risk. Much of modern Christianity and Judaism has, rightly or wrongly, lost this sense of God as terrifying power and frightening mystery, and of this aspect of God's anger. But what must not be lost, at any cost, is the other sense of God's anger at evil and at human sin. This is the "anger" in question in Psalm 103. This is also what the "visiting the iniquity of the parents upon the children" in Exodus 20:6 and 34:7 is about. This is what many versions of the New Testament know as the "wrath of God", or as some modern ones sometimes call it, his "anger" or his "retribution".

The Old Testament is fully aware of shadow sides of human life, one of which is human "iniquity". It is fully aware of how damaging such "iniquity", "sin" or "wickedness" can be, and it does not think that it is something to be treated lightly or dismissed easily. The Old Testament prophets insisted that sin, in all of its chameleon colours, makes God "angry", because it fouls up his creation and spoils life for its victims. Where there should be love there is hatred, despair where hope should be, darkness where light should be and where there should be joy there is sadness. There is also injury, and so doubt has become inevitable, as St Francis points out in his famous prayer. In the face of all this it would be a very poor God indeed who did not get angry. Anyone who looks at the misery of so many people and so much of our planet and feels neither pain nor rage can hardly be human, and a God who was not angry at the cause of these things would be less than human. The God of the Bible is angry because he sees what has happened to his creation and feels for the victims of the injustices of the powerful, for "he has made nothing in vain and loves all that he has made" (from the Burial Service). Only a heartless and unloving God would not get angry. Just as good parents can get angry when they see their child hurting themselves and hurting others, so God's anger is, in fact, a sign of his love.

However, he is "slow to anger", or patient with sinful people. He does not nurse his anger, or let it go on and on. God's anger is a sign that he takes sin and evil seriously, hating their devastating effects on human life and the life of the world. It is not however, his last or greatest word, for that lies with his love which seeks to put all things right and to which Exodus 34:5-9 so beautifully testifies.

Note

Number 16 in the psalms found in the Dead Sea Scrolls at Qumran

> "I know, O Lord,
> that Thou art merciful and compassionate,
> long-suffering and rich in grace and truth,
> pardoning transgression and sin.
> Thou repentest of evil against them that love Thee,
> and keep Thy commandments,
> that return to thee with faith
> and wholeness of heart..."
>
> from *The Dead Sea Scrolls in English*
> by G Vermes, JSOT Press, 1987, p204

Also published by
SOUTHLEIGH PUBLICATIONS

Why Bible-Believing Methodists shouldn't eat Black Pudding
The Bible what is it? how did we get it? how shall we use it?

(Revised edition)

Stephen B Dawes

Too often the question about the authority of the Bible is addressed without taking *theBible as it is* and *how it has come to us* seriously enough. This book looks at those two areas before it talks about *how to use* the Bible.

It is written out of the conviction that simply saying,"The Bible says ..." and insisting that the Bible is the supreme authority for the Christian does not take the Bible as it is or the Church which created it seriously enough.

ISBN 0 952064 7 2   1996   84pp   £2 (inc p&p)

Desert Island Hymns
Faith which sings with heart and mind

Stephen B Dawes

This is not just a book about favourite hymns. In it Stephen Dawes discusses the eight hymns which for him best sum up what it means to be a Christian and which he thinks best take us to the heart of the Christian Faith. They are *How sweet the name of Jesus sounds; Cradled in a manger, meanly; When I survey; I know that my Redeemer lives; May the mind of Christ my Saviour; Fill Thou my life; Being of beings, God of love* and *God is here!*

ISBN 0 9520644 6 4   1996   97pp   £3.50 (inc p&p)